Battleground

The Wars of the Roses

FROM WAKEFIELD TO TOWTON

Other guides in the Battleground Europe Series:

Walking the Salient *by* Paul Reed
Ypres - Sanctuary Wood and Hooge *by* Nigel Cave
Ypres - Hill 60 *by* Nigel Cave
Ypres - Messines Ridge *by* Peter Oldham
Ypres - Polygon Wood *by* Nigel Cave
Ypres - Passchendaele *by* Nigel Cave
Ypres - Airfields and Airmen *by* Michael O'Connor
Ypres - St Julien *by* Graham Keech

Walking the Somme *by* Paul Reed
Somme - Gommecourt *by* Nigel Cave
Somme - Serre *by* Jack Horsfall & Nigel Cave
Somme - Beaumont Hamel *by* Nigel Cave
Somme - Thiepval *by* Michael Stedman
Somme - La Boisselle *by* Michael Stedman
Somme - Fricourt *by* Michael Stedman
Somme - Carnoy-Montauban *by* Graham Maddocks
Somme - Pozieres *by* Graham Keech
Somme - Courcelette *by* Paul Reed
Somme - Boom Ravine *by* Trevor Pidgeon
Somme - Mametz Wood *by* Michael Renshaw
Somme - Delville Wood *by* Nigel Cave
Somme - Advance to Victory (North) 1918 *by* Michael Stedman
Somme - Flers *by* Trevor Pidgeon
Somme - Bazentin Ridge *by* Edward Hancock and Nigel Cave
Somme - Combles *by* Paul Reed

Arras - Vimy Ridge *by* Nigel Cave
Arras - Gavrelle *by* Trevor Tasker and Kyle Tallett
Arras - Bullecourt *by* Graham Keech
Arras - Monchy le Preux *by* Colin Fox

Hindenburg Line *by* Peter Oldham
Hindenburg Line Epehy *by* Bill Mitchinson
Hindenburg Line Riqueval *by* Bill Mitchinson
Hindenburg Line Villers-Plouich *by* Bill Mitchinson
Hindenburg Line - Cambrai *by* Jack Horsfall & Nigel Cave
Hindenburg Line - Saint Quentin *by* Helen McPhail and Philip Guest

La Bassée - Neuve Chapelle *by* Geoffrey Bridger
Mons *by* Jack Horsfall and Nigel Cave
Accrington Pals Trail *by* William Turner

Poets at War: Wilfred Owen *by* Helen McPhail and Philip Gues
Poets at War: Edmund Blunden *by* Helen McPhail and Philip Gu
Poets at War: Graves & Sassoon *by* Helen McPhail and Philip G

Gallipoli *by* Nigel Steel

Italy - Asiago *by* Francis Mackay

Boer War - The Relief of Ladysmith *by* Lewis Childs
Boer War - The Siege of Ladysmith *by* Lewis Childs
Boer War - Kimberley *by* Lewis Childs
Isandlwana *by* Ian Knight and Ian Castle
Rorkes Drift *by* Ian Knight and Ian Castle

Napoleonic - Hougoumont *by* Julian Paget and Derek Saunders

Wars of the Roses **- Wakefield/ Towton** *by* Philip A. Haigh

WW2 **Pegasus Bridge/Merville Battery** *by* Carl Shilleto
WW2 **Utah Beach** *by* Carl Shilleto
WW2 **Gold Beach** *by* Christopher Dunphie & Garry Johnson
WW2 **Omaha Beach** *by* Tim Kilvert-Jones
WW2 **Sword Beach** *by* Tim Kilvert-Jones
WW2 **Battle of the Bulge - St Vith** *by* Michael Tolhurst
WW2 **Battle of the Bulge - Bastogne** *by* Michael Tolhurst
WW2 **Dunkirk** *by* Patrick Wilson
WW2 **Calais** *by* Jon Cooksey
WW2 **Boulogne** *by* Jon Cooksey
WW2 ***Das Reich*** **– Drive to Normandy** *by* Philip Vickers
WW2 **Hill 112** *by* Tim Saunders
WW2 **Market Garden - Nijmegen** *by* Tim Saunders
WW2 **Market Garden - Hell's Highway** *by* Tim Saunders
WW2 **Market Garden - Arnhem** *by* Frank Steer
WW2 **Normandy - Jig Beach** *by* Tim Saunders

Battleground Europe Series guides under contract for future release:

Somme - High Wood *by* Terry Carter
Somme - German Advance 1918 *by* Michael Stedman
Somme - Beaucourt *by* Michael Renshaw
Walking Arras *by* Paul Reed
WW2 **Channel Islands** *by* George Forty
WW2 **Market Garden - The Island** *by* Tim Saunders
Touring the Italian Front - *by* Francis Mackay
Civil War - Naseby *by* Martin Marix Evans, Peter Burton, Michael Westa

Battleground England

The Wars of the Roses

FROM WAKEFIELD TO TOWTON

PHILIP A HAIGH

LEO COOPER

First published in 2002
by LEO COOPER
an imprint of
Pen & Sword Books Limited
47 Church Street, Barnsley, South Yorkshire S70 2AS

ISBN 0 85052 825 9

A CIP catalogue record of this book is available
from the British Library

Printed by CPI UK

For up-to-date information on other titles produced under the Leo Cooper imprint, please telephone or write to:

Pen & Sword Books Ltd, FREEPOST, 47 Church Street
Barnsley, South Yorkshire S70 2AS
Telephone 01226 734222

CONTENTS

Signatures of the two brothers, Edward Earl of March and Edmund Earl of Rutland, in a letter to their father, Richard Duke of York. There was just over a year difference in their ages, and they were very close. The youngest, Edmund, aged seventeen was murdered at Wakefield Bridge following the Battle of Wakefield in which their father, the Duke of York, was slain in 1460. Edward avenged their deaths at the Battle of Towton just three months later.

Introduction

When I was asked to complete this work, I considered carefully the fact that instinctively, when people think of Yorkshire and the Wars of the Roses, they think only of the battle of Towton. Scarcely given a second thought, are the smaller, but no less interesting – and in some cases significant – battles at Wakefield and Ferrybridge.

To overcome the fact that the Wars of the Roses in Yorkshire contained not only the battle of Towton, but these other engagements too, then this work was written. It explores each in turn and allows the reader to explore yesterdays battlefields today – with the aid of a 'tour' – using modern day roads and footpaths. As always, in order to describe the military aspects of the Wars of the Roses, you must first tackle the events that led up to and resulted from them – and indeed their long term consequences. The reader should therefore be aware, that this is a work about military history and that therein lies the focus of this work, not the political intrigue that surrounded the battles themsleves.

Consequently, the history of the wars – and the events between each engagement – are left intentionally brief, to ensure that the military aspects of the Wars of the Roses in Yorkshire are covered in detail. However, for those who wish to have a more detailed knowledge of these political events, then there are many references to other works throughout this one, that will direct such students of history to the relevant places to find the information they require. On the subject of other works, I would like the reader to be aware that I'm not a believer in reinventing the wheel, and in writing this work, I have reviewed, as far as I am aware, much if not all of the documentation available on the actual battles and the battlefields themselves. In many instances throughout, I have, as in previous works, quoted from the authors of other books and journals, both contemporary, near contemporary and modern day, in the completion of my own. I make no apology for this, as many of these earlier writers, were, and still are, specialists in their own field, and as such, they are more qualified than I to make an assessment of a particular aspect from the battles detailed in this work. Therefore, it would be wrong for me to try and compete with them, and even more remiss of me to take their work and words as my own.

Finally, I would like to share with you the fact that it has always been my desire to see an all embracing series of works on the subject of the military aspects of the Wars of the Roses. As such, it is my hope that this work will be followed by several others, written in the same format, that will allow the many thousands of people interested in war and the Wars of the Roses, to walk all the battlefields from this period of our history sufficiently armed with information to discover today, who did what, where and when, yesterday – and more importantly why.

Acknowledgements

I would like to thank the following people for their help and support in bringing this work to its conclusion. First and foremost my wife Sarah and my children Lewis and Charlotte – once again I'm indebted for their patience and understanding. The staff of both Leeds and Wakefield Libraries, for supplying many previously produced, but out of print articles and works regarding the battles of Wakefield, Ferrybridge and Towton – I never cease to be amazed by their patience, knowledge and willingness to help. In regard to this, I would particularly like to thank Ms Jennifer Horne of Leeds Library, without whose efforts, on my behalf, much of the supporting documentation required to produce this work would have been very difficult and certainly time consuming to find.

I would also like to thank my fellow historians, Andrew Boardman, Dave Cooke and Graham Bell, for enlightening me to some facts hitherto unknown to me regarding the battles of Wakefield, Ferrybridge and Towton. On that latter note, I would also like to thank Geoffrey Wheeler for his kindly help regarding the content of this work and for the illustrations in this finished book. Photographs supplied by Geoff are marked GW.

Also, Christie's of London, in particular Mr David Williams, for supplying the photograph of the 'Wakefield Sword' and granting permission for its use in this work. I would also like to thank my friends and colleagues – particularly those who have had to suffer my many battlefield analogies during the time we have spent together – for their on-going support in particlulary Kevin Shenton, Deborah-Jane Higginson, Michael Fellows, Lee Thornton and Mo Asif – who has been especially supportive through what has been a difficult period of my life – thank you Mo.

Philip A. Haigh

Series Designer's acknowledgements

With over sixty titles in the **Battleground** series of guide books covering conflicts in France, Belgium, Holland, Turkey, South Africa, and the United States of America, the time has arrived for us to apply the successful formula to the battlefields of Britain. *From Wakefield to Towton* by Philip Haigh is the first title in the *Battleground Britain* sub series. This particular subject was chosen to launch the series because of the fascinating aspects in this account of The Wars of the Roses. Usually regarded as a complicated, bloody affair between the houses of Lancaster and York lasting some thirty years and which witnessed much changing of sides, the events bracketed by Christmas 1460 (Wakefield) and Palm Sunday 1461 (Towton), are refreshingly clear. A manipulative woman married to a weak King – Henry VI – representing the House of Lancaster and pitted against a seemingly decent chap, the Duke of York; battles, betrayals, pitiless murder, beheading, ridicule and disgrace, revenge and the crowning of a Yorkist king – Edward IV. Surely, this is an interesting period in the history of England with which to begin the new series.

In directing this work I have been assisted by the following organisations and individuals: Pam Judkins, Keeper of Archaeology, Wakefield; Steve Coulson, Pontefract Castle; Kate Taylor, Wakefield Historical Publications; Christine Varney, Conisbrough Castle; Maurice Hepworth, Barnsley Libraries Archives and Local Studies. Also members of the Towton Battlefield Society and members of The Retinue of Sir Thomas Stanley. Special thanks must go to Ken Everitt for his active support of this project and his phenomenal knowledge of this period in our history.

Roni Wilkinson (November 2001)

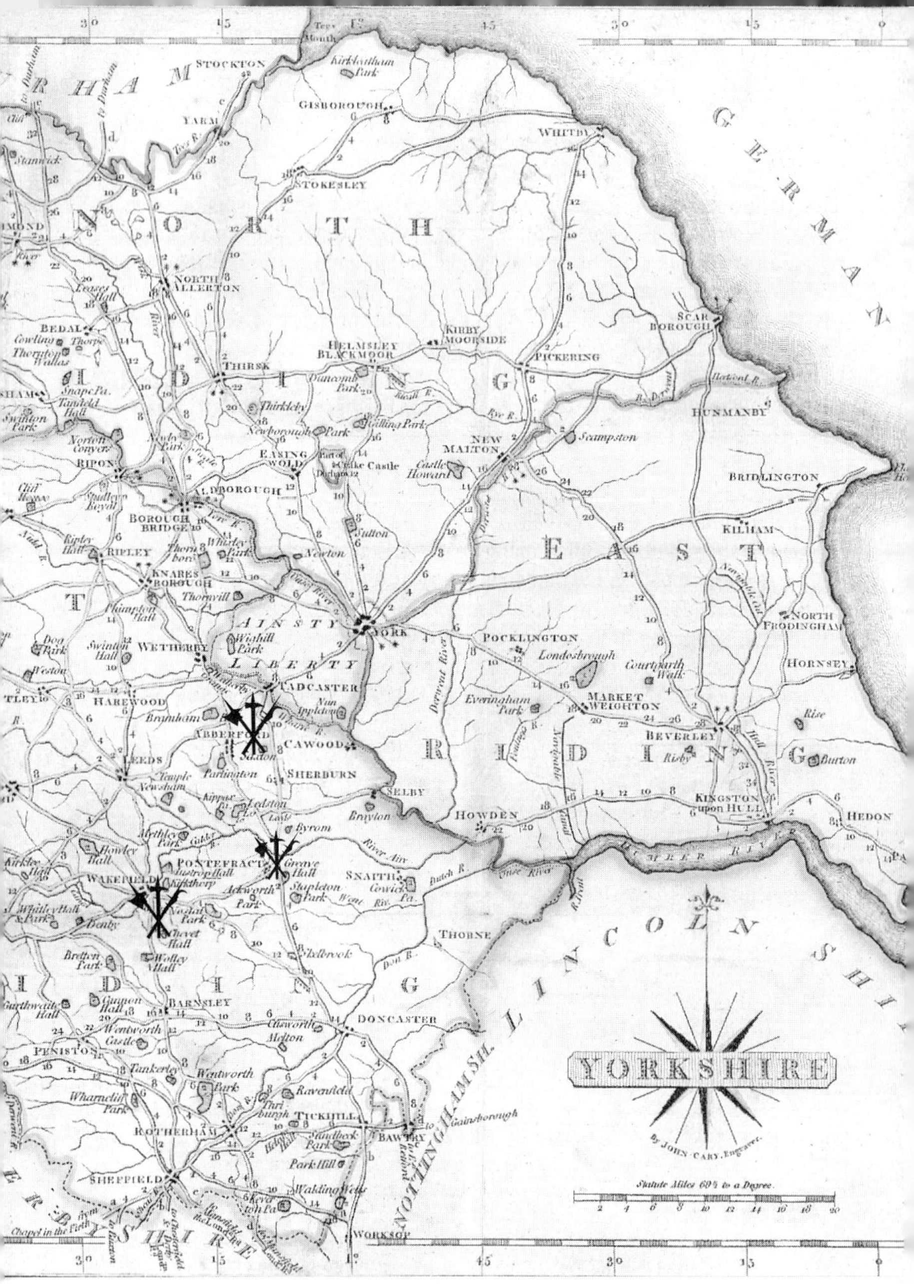

Locations of the the battles fought in Yorkshire between Christmas week 146 (Wakefield) and March 29, Palm Sunday 1461 (Towton), by the Houses of Lancaste and York. The antagonists being the reigning monarch, King Henry VI and Quee Margaret for the House of Lancaster, and Richard Duke of York (who was killed Wakefield) and King Edward IV (acclaimed king in March, 1461) for the House of Yor

Chapter One

The Origins of the Wars of the Roses

Family feuding

ON THE MORNING of 3 March 1452, at Blackheath, near London, two armed forces faced each other prepared to commence battle, a battle which would have been – had it not been averted – the first engagement in what would, in later years, become known as the Wars of the Roses. This entire encounter was recorded in the *London Chronicle* and is reported as follows:

> 'The 30th year of King Henry the Sixth. This year on Wednesday the 16th day of February the king with the lords rode towards the Duke of York for to take him, because he raised people to come down and take the Duke of Somerset; but when the Duke of York heard here of, he took another way and so came towards London. And also soon the king heard here of, he sent letters to the mayor, alderman and commons of London, on St Mathies' day, that they should keep the city and suffer not the Duke of York to come therein; wherefore was made great watch in the city, the which was told the Duke of York, wherefore he left London way and went over Kingston Bridge. And on the Monday after, in the morning they were removed from thence into

The Duke of Somerset, at King Henry's right hand denounces The Duke of York as a traitor. Richard counter-charges Somerset with treasonous intent whilst the King sits incapable of dealing with the bitter rivals.

The Wars of the Roses

Clearly, even today, there seems to be a misunderstanding regarding the use of the names Yorkist and Lancastrian in context with the Wars of the Roses. Unlike the modern day cricket match, the term 'Wars of the Roses', does not reflect a geographical conflict between the County of Yorkshire and the County of Lancaster. In fact, the term 'Wars of the Roses' refers to a dynastic struggle between the House of Lancaster – the supporters of Henry VI and his heirs – and the House of York – the supporters of Richard, Duke of York and his heirs. Indeed, the reference to roses refers to the symbols that Shakespeare (in *Henry VI*) would have us believe (and now immortalised in the painting by Henry Payne), that each side chose as their emblems a rose – that is a white rose for the Yorkists, and the red rose for the Lancastrians. It was only after the event that the conflict was credited with the title the 'Wars of the Roses', allegedly christened as such by Sir Walter Scott, (see the introduction to Lander's, *The Wars of the Roses*). However, if the 'Wars of the Roses' is to be given any sort of geographical boundaries, then it could, loosely, be described as a north/south conflict. The reason for this is due to the fact that the supporters of the House of Lancaster held lands predominately to the north (including the majority of the County of Lancashire and Yorkshire and Northumberland) while the supporters of the House of York held lands along the south coast, Kent etc, East Anglia and in the Midlands. This was to be a particular problem for the Duke of York during the Wakefield Campaign, due to the fact that while he owned Sandal, the surrounding lands were predominatly held by supporters of the House of Lancaster.

The plucking of the red and white roses in the Old Temple Gardens, by Henry Payne, immortalising the scene from Shakespeare's Henry VI, where opposing factions declare their loyalties by selecting either a red rose, representing the House of Lancaster, or a white rose for the House of York. GW

Kent. And at afternoon the same day the king came to London with his host, and so went into Southwark and lodged at St Mary Overeys. And the Duke of York pitched his field about Dartford with great ordnance. And whilst the king lay still at St Mary Overeys bishops rode between the king and the Duke of York to set them at rest and peace.

'But the Duke of York said he would have the Duke of Somerset, or else he would die therefore. And on Wednesday next following (1 March) the king with his host rode to Blackheath, and forth over Shooters' Hill to Welling, and there lodged that day and the morrow. And on Thursday at afternoon there was made a pointment between the king and the Duke of York by the mean of lords and on the morrow, that was Friday, the king assembled his host on the Blackheath afore noon; and there abode the coming of the Duke of York after pointment made over even. And in the king's host was numbered 20,000 fighting men, and men said the Duke of York had as many with much great stuff and ordnance. And at the last the Duke of York came with forty horse to the king about noon, and obeyed him to his liegance; and with (him) the Earl of Devonshire and the Lord Cobham, the which held the Duke of York and were in host with him. And the king took them to grace and all.' [1]

Henry VI a weak, saintly character, influenced by his beautiful, strong-willed wife Margaret of Anjou.

What the chronicle does not tell us, is that when York entered the king's tent, expecting to take the Duke of Somerset into custody, he found him, despite the king's previous promise to hand Somerset over into York's custody on the king's right hand side and – not surprisingly – himself under arrest. York was held prisoner for three months, and it was only after he swore an oath of allegiance, at St. Paul's Cathedral, never to raise arms against the king again, that he was allowed to go free.

To understand why it was that the King, Henry VI, and the realm's most powerful noble, Richard, Duke of York, should face each other in such a manner, we must return to the year 1411. It was in this year, that Richard Plantagenet was born to Richard, fifth Earl of Cambridge and Anne Mortimer. His father was the son of Edmund, the first Duke of York, who was in turn the fourth son of Edward III.

If Henry VI had died before 1453, the year of the birth of Edward, Prince of Wales, then Richard would have undoubtedly been crowned King of England. There was no other noble, since the death of Henry VI's uncle, the Duke of Gloucester, with such a strong claim to the throne than Richard.

Being so highly placed in the royal household, Richard was destined to play a significant role in the Government and politics of England throughout his lifetime and in England's affairs in France during the later stages of the Hundred Years War. He was appointed Lieutenant of France in 1436. Throughout his service in Europe, he had to pay for the services of his men and finance the army in France from his own personal funds.

York was a wealthy man in his own right. He was the sole benefactor of the childless Edmund Mortimer who had died of plague in Ireland in 1425. His marriage to 'The Rose of Raby', Cicely Neville, in 1438, daughter to Ralph Neville, Earl of Westmoreland and sister of Richard Neville, Earl of Salisbury, had brought him great wealth. Thus he was able to fund the English army overseas, though unhappy to do so. By the time he left France, York had forwarded some £38,000 of his own money to maintain English interests in France. To add insult to injury, in 1445 he was replaced as Lieutenant of France by Edmund Beaufort, Duke of Somerset. It is not to be doubted that it was on Somerset's advice (Henry VI's cousin, and someone Henry trusted more than the Duke of York) that Henry VI created York Lieutenant of Ireland, which was in reality, exile by office. Somerset was no doubt fearful of York, a fear enhanced by the fact that Somerset, a man whom York equally detested, and a favourite of Henry VI was forwarded funds to the sum of £25,000 to sustain the king's army in France.

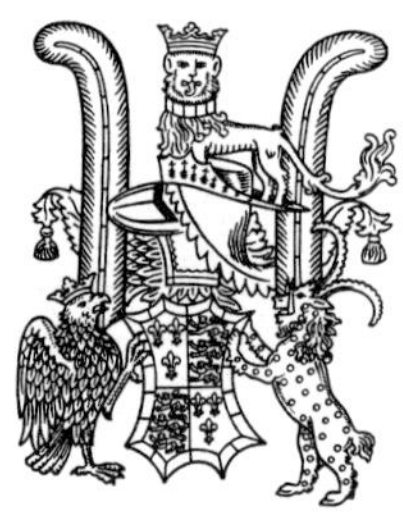

Badge of the Duke of Somerset

Badge of the Duke of York

Not only did York detest Somerset because he was the the King's favourite but he also did not much like the fact that Somerset had been given the office the Duke had previously held in France along with the necessary funds to support it, despite his inability as a soldier. York's fears over the management of the campaign in France were realised, when very soon the war began to go badly for the English. The Duke of Somerset was personally responsible for the surrender of the strategic town of Rouen which subsequently led to the fall of Normandy to Charles VII of France. Because of this, Somerset became distinctly unpopular at home. However, because he retained the king's favour, he maintained his prestigious position at court.

In June 1451 Bordeaux and Gascony were lost to the French. This was disastrous news for the English and the King, Henry VI, took the loss very badly. York in turn, was quick to blame Somerset for the disaster and, with support for the king and his adherents at such a low point (due mainly to English failings in France), York, decided to risk all and attempt to wrest

THE HOUSES OF YORK AND LANCASTER

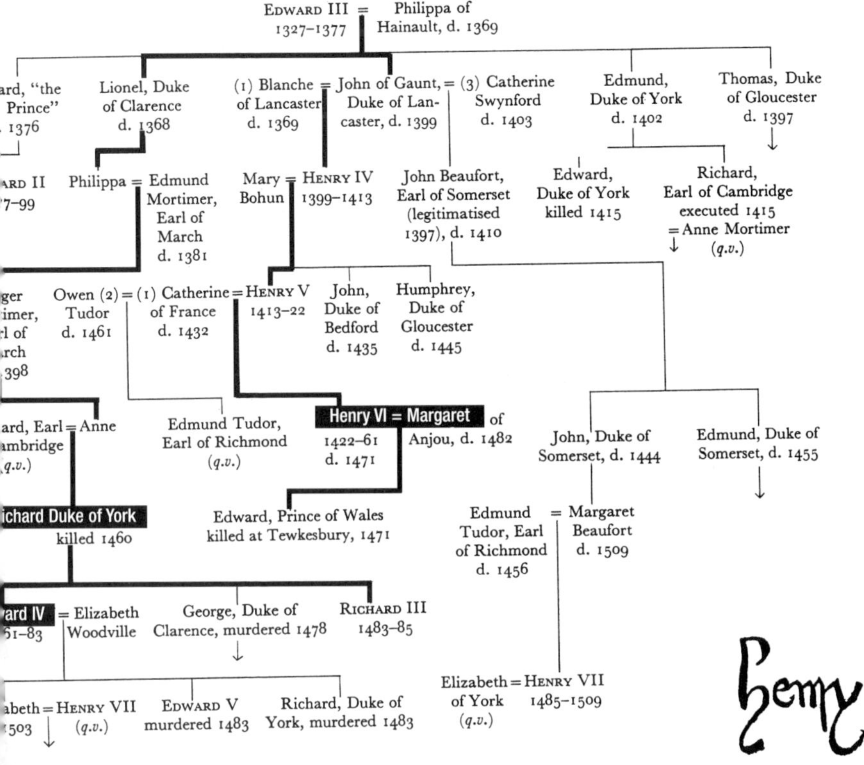

Two branches of the same family tree – the houses of Lancaster and York – related by blood but divided by ambition, fought each other for the throne of England.

control from the king by force of arms and arrest the Duke of Somerset, thus removing him from his position as the king's most senior advisor.

Doubtless this move was not only inspired by York's fear for the conduct of the war in France, but also because he was equally fearful that Somerset might take over the very position that York felt was his own, that of the most likely heir to Henry in the absence of the king having any children of his own. Thus York, believing that he had more popular support than he actually had, sailed from Ireland and landed in North Wales, gathered his forces and travelled straight for London and the encounter at Blackheath.

The Wars of the Roses begin

After York's release from custody, there then followed several years of relative peace. However, by the year 1453, the political storm clouds were once again gathering over the country. At this time, England's possessions in

France had been almost lost as the disastrous Hundred Years War had all but come to an end. It was this – it is said – that brought about the first bout of madness in Henry VI. What form this illness took is not recorded, but it seems that it manifested itself in a form of paralysis. York, with the king incapacitated, was made protector of England and took the opportunity to seek revenge on his earlier enemies, namely the Duke of Somerset, who was sent to the Tower on a revised charge of treason (for his poor management of the war in France) in September 1453. The Earl of Salisbury, Richard Neville and his eldest son Richard, Earl of Warwick, also took the opportunity afforded by the king's illness and, under the cover of their kinsman's protectorate began to seek their revenge against the Percy family, the Earls of Northumberland, with whom they had held a long running feud, over the issue of ownership of property in Northumberland and Yorkshire.

Thus, England was plunged into a series of minor wars between the land's most powerful lords to which the Duke of York, as protector, was able to use his authority to the advantage of his family and supporters. However, this all came to an end when the king recovered from his illness in January 1455. Somerset was released from the Tower, and immediately formed a natural alliance with Henry Percy, Earl of Northumberland and with Percy's ally in the north Lord Clifford, against the Duke of York – who was stripped of his powers as protector – and his supporters, namely the Earl of Salisbury and the Earl of Warwick. With this the battle lines for the 'Wars of the Roses' were drawn. The pact between Somerset, Northumberland and Clifford, supported by the king would in later years go by the name of Lancastrians, taken from the family name of the House of Lancaster from which the lineage of Henry VI was derived. While the followers of the House of York, Warwick, Salisbury and the Duke of York himself became known as the Yorkists.

The first Battle of St. Albans

The Duke of York realised that he would soon become the target of Lancastrian hostility now that he had been removed from the office of protector, and as such returned to his estates in the north to consider what would be the best course of action to take. His fears were soon realised when a council meeting was planned to be held at Leicester 21 May 1455, to which he was asked to attend alone without his supporters and troops. York realised it was a trap, and gathered his forces and those of the Earls of Salisbury and Warwick together and marched south to confront the king. What transpired immediately after this was chronicled as follows:

> 'When the Duke of Somerset and those who were of his party then being in the City of London, heard that the Duke of York and many other lords in his company were advancing against them with a force of five thousand men and when considered what he had done against the said Duke of York and that he was also in very bad odour with the people of London, he came to the conclusion that he would fall upon him the moment he [the Duke of York] arrived. For which cause he

Richard, Duke of York, bears the Sovereign's sword during a procession through the streets of London. Henry VI had growing concerns as to Richard's loyalty to him and his House.

persuaded the king to sally forth against the Duke of York and his other enemies, their opponents, and hastily gathered the said third day after the feast of Ascension up to 3,500 persons and on the 21st day of May in the morning [they] issued out of London and went to lodge twenty miles away from there at a little village where there is an abbey called St. Albans, near which village at less than half a day's march their enemies were lodged.

These, when they knew of the king's coming, immediately approached him and also the 22nd day of the said month very early the king sent a herald to the Duke of York to know the cause for which he had come there with so many men and that it seemed to the king something quite new that he, the duke, should be rising against him, the king. The reply made was that he was not coming against him thus, [he]

> was always ready to do him obedience but he well intended in one way or another to have the traitors who were about him so that they should be punished, and that in case he could not have them with good will and fair consent, he intended in any case to have them by force.'[2]

With this, the parley ended and the battle began. The Yorkists attempted to gain access to the fortified town of St. Albans by attacking the town gates located on Sopwell Lane and Shropshire Lane. However, it was only an attack through the 'Back Gardens' the piece of ground located between the aforementioned gates, by the Earl of Warwick's men commanded by Sir Robert Ogle, that broke the deadlock and ended the battle with the defeat of the Lancastrians, the capture of the king, and the death of the Earl of Northumberland, Henry Percy, the Duke of Somerset, Edmund Beaufort and Lord Clifford of Craven. The scene was thus set for the bitter feuding to follow.

The king, who was captured during the battle and now enjoyed the 'protection' of his Yorkist cousins, returned to London the next day and entered the city with great pomp and ceremony, with York riding on his right, the Earl of Salisbury to his left, while the Earl of Warwick rode a little ahead bearing the royal sword.

The Battle of Blore Heath

Putting St. Albans behind him, the Duke of York, having achieved this 'coup', was again made protector of the realm for the second time. However, this came to an end in February 1456, when the king, no doubt inspired by the tenacious nature of his wife, Margaret of Anjou, announced that he was able to rule in his own right. He threw off the shackles of his Yorkist adversaries and set about trying to re-impose his rule over the kingdom.

In reality, it was Queen Margaret, Henry VI's wife, who was the main fomenter of the Lancastrian resurgence, and it was she, in Henry's name, who instigated the removal of all Yorkist supporters from offices of state which had been given to them by the Duke of York in his time as protector of the realm. With this, the Duke of York and the Earl of Salisbury once again 'retreated' to their estates in the north. The queen was determined to rid her and the king, of Yorkist undertones once and for all and as such arranged for a council meeting to be held in the name of the king, which was planned to convene at Coventry. At this meeting, in June 1459, all the great nobles of the land were instructed to attend. However, York, Salisbury and Warwick (the earl, who at this point had returned from Calais) were not invited, and Margaret planned to have them all charged with acts of treason against the king and the state.

York, realising what was at stake, arranged the union of his forces, and sent word to the Earl of Salisbury – who was at Middleham – and the Earl of Warwick – who was in London – to meet with him near York's stronghold at Ludlow. The Lancastrians however, were not unaware of what the duke was planning and moves were made to intercept them. It was only a force under the command of John Touchet, Lord Audley. His army came across the forces of the Earl of Salisbury on 23 September 1459, at Blore Heath, near Newcastle under Lyme. Again, as in the battle of St.albans, for those who want an understanding of the campaign and battle of Blore Heath, I suggest that the following should be consulted. A. H. Burne's, *More Battlefields of England*, Methuen, 1952, (pages 140 – 149), and the recent publication of, *The Battle of Blore Heath 1459*, Ed Paddy Griffith, Paddy Griffith Associates, 1995 – as this work includes a reprint of an original work – dated 1912 – by Colonel F. R. Twemlow.

Earl of Warwick, the most powerful man in England, and supporter of Richard of York. Painted by a Tudor artist.

The Yorkists were the victors in the battle of Blore Heath, and a short while later they managed to join together with York and Warwick at Ludford Bridge near Ludlow, but it was at this place that treachery was first to show its hand. A contingent of the Earl of Warwick's men, under the command of Andrew Trollope, their captain, acting on a promise of pardon given by Henry VI, deserted to the Lancastrians, causing the remaining Yorkist commanders to lose heart. They were now faced with such overwhelming opposition that they planned their escape. Under the pretence of returning to Ludlow Castle for the night, the Yorkist commanders fled. The Duke of York, taking the Earl of Rutland with him, returned to the safety of Ireland while the Earl of Warwick, Earl of Salisbury and Edward, Earl of March, fled to the safety of Calais.

With this, it would appear that the Yorkist cause had come to an end, especially after the Yorkist commanders were formally 'attainted' and declared traitors at a Parliament held at Coventry in November. However, the Lancastrians did not count on the tenacity and courage of the Earl of Warwick whose actions in the coming months were to turn the fortunes of the wars once again, in the Yorkists favour.

Although trapped in Calais, the Earl of Warwick, who was as much at home at sea as he was on dry land, was soon conducting pirate-style raids on passing shipping and no doubt planning the revival of the Yorkist cause on mainland England. To assist with this, Warwick sailed to Ireland in the

March of 1460 to confer with the Duke of York and plan the Yorkist return to power. Calais, which was left under the command of the Earls of Salisbury and March, was soon placed under siege by a Lancastrian force under the command of the son of Edmund Beaufort, Henry, who was now the new Duke of Somerset.

However, the fortress remained resolute, and the Duke of Somerset had to withdraw to the nearby fortress at Guines. With Warwick's return to Calais in May 1460, it appears that the Yorkists' plans for the 'invasion' of England were complete.

Heralds in the background signal the commencement of battle in this fanciful depiction of mediaeval warfare, which includes bowmen, pikemen and cavalry.

The Battle of Northampton

On 26 June 1460, the Earl of Warwick along with the Earls of Salisbury and March landed at Sandwich with a small army and proceeded to march for London. This Yorkist force was soon joined by many followers from Kent, where the Yorkist commanders had remained popular, and promptly arrived at the capital. Meanwhile, the Lancastrians were gathering at Coventry and Warwick.

The Earl of Warwick, his army increasing in numbers all the time, was eager to bring them into battle. The two forces met at Northampton on 10 July 1460. The battle that was fought there was described by the author of *An English Chronicle of the reigns of Richard II, Henry IV, V, VI* as follows:

> 'The king at Northampton lay at Friars and had ordained there a strong and a mighty field, in the meadows beside the nunnery, armed and arrayed with guns, having the river at his back. The earls with the number of 60,000, as it was said, came to Northampton and sent certain bishops to the king beseeching him that in eschewing of effusion of Christian blood he would admit and suffer the earls to come to his presence to declare them self as they were.
>
> 'The Duke of Buckingham that stood beside the king, said unto them, "Ye come not as Bishops for to treat for peace, but as men of arms"; because they brought with them a notable company of men at arms. They answered and said, "We come thus for surety of our persons, for they that be-eth about the king be-eth not our friends." "Forsooth" said the duke, "the Earl of Warwick shall not come to the king's presence, and if he come he shall die." The messengers returned again, and told this to the earls...
>
> '...Then on the Thursday the 10 of July, the year of Our Lord 1460, at two hours after noon, the said Earls of March and Warwick let cry through the field, that no man should lay a hand on the king ne on the common people, but only on the lords, knights and squires: then trumpets blew up, and both hosts countered and fought together half an hour. The Lord Grey, that was the king's vaward, broke the field and came to the earl's (Warwick and Edward's) party which caused the salvation of many a man's life: many were slain, and many were fled, and were drowned in the river.' [3]

With this, the battle ended and the Lancastrian rout began.

The Act of Accord

Once more, King Henry, who was again captured after the battle, found himself under the 'protection' of the Yorkists, and the Earl of Warwick immediately ordered the return to London so that the Yorkist commanders could set about bringing Yorkist control once again to the realm. Throughout, the Duke of York had remained in Ireland. However, early in September he landed at Chester and made a leisurely tour of the Welsh

Marches before travelling to London. Upon his arrival in the capital, York ordered that trumpets be sounded and that his sword should be held before him as he marched to Westminster, where many of the lords of the land had gathered to await his arrival. Abbot Whethamstede of St. Albans abbey takes up the story:

> 'And coming there he walked straight on, until he came to the king's throne, upon the covering or cushion on which laying his hand, in this very act like a man about to take possession of his right, he held it upon it for a short time. But at length withdrawing it, he turned his face to the people, standing quietly under the canopy of royal state, he looked eagerly for their applause.
>
> 'While however, he was standing thus and turning his face to the people and while he was judging their applause, Master Thomas Bourchier Archbishop of Canterbury, rose up and having exchanged greetings asked if he would come and see the king. He, as if stung in soul by this question, replied shortly: "I do not recall that I know anyone within the kingdom whom it would not befit to come sooner to me and see me rather than I should go visit him."
>
> 'The archbishop having heard this reply, quickly withdrew, and reported to the king, the answer which he had heard from the duke's mouth. While the archbishop was thus withdrawing, he too retired to the principal apartments of the whole palace...' [4]

It is clear that the duke had, until this point, felt that he had the overwhelming support of the lords and nobles who were present. However, as the previous quote clearly demonstrates, York had once again failed to comprehend the true reality of the political situation and had overestimated the level of support he actually had. The reason for this was probably that the lords were disillusioned with the fact that York had remained in Ireland for so long and left the Earl of Warwick to lead the Yorkist campaign in England. Also, it is likely that the lords and nobles of the land, although despairing at Henry VI's weak rule, were, nevertheless, equally aware that Henry was their king. The thought of supporting York in actually replacing him as their sovereign lord, though no doubt appealing to many, still required them and the Duke of York to break their oaths to serve the king and in Richard's case, never again to take up arms against the king. This went beyond what they felt they could openly support with honour – in this supposed chivalrous age.

The Earl of Warwick, it appears, was aware of this feeling and as John de Waurin later chronicled, was furious with the Duke of York and his actions since his return to England. Shortly after this event he went to the duke:

> '...and there were angry words for the earl showed the duke how the lords and people were ill content against him because he wished to strip the king of his crown.' [5]

However, York was undaunted and set about pressing home his claim to rule the country by legal means. To that end, in a meeting of the Lords and the Commons on 7 October 1460, Parliament recognised York's position, and on the 24 October, Parliament passed the 'Act of Accord' – in which it was

Richard Duke of York dropped all pretence of supporting King Henry VI when, in September 1460, he marched into London and indicated that he expected to be acclaimed the Ruler of England. Unfortunately for him his timing was wrong – the support was not there.

agreed that Henry would remain king until his death, and only then would the crown pass to the Duke of York or his heirs.

Clearly, the Act of Accord was a direct result of the Lancastrian defeat at the battle of Northampton. This point was not lost on the modern day historian, Anthony Goodman, who wrote in his own work titled, *The Wars of the Roses*, the following regarding it:

> 'The consequences of the battle of Northampton differed greatly from those of the first battle of St. Albans. The latter had so shocked contemporaries that it has ushered in a period of political compromise, leading eventually to the new court ascendancy against which York rebelled in 1459. But the compromise after Northampton rested on a novel, even more unstable basis – the recognition of Yorkist dynastic claims. York's acceptance as Henry's heir in the Parliament in October immediately provoked a struggle for the crown, a war of succession, producing widespread involvement and lasting bitterness as it developed into what some contemporaries regarded as a war of the north against the south. Once the dynastic issue had been raised, with such dramatic and extreme consequences, it was hard to bottle up again...' [6]

As such, further conflict was inevitable.

Chapter Two

The 1460 Campaign

The march from London

THE REASON WHY it can be claimed that it was the Act of Accord, ratified on 24 October 1460, which brought about the battle of Wakefield, is as follows: although this constitutional settlement was acceptable to the Yorkists, it certainly did not sit well with the Lancastrians. Queen Margaret in particular was opposed to it, because of the fact that it forfeited the birthright of her child, Prince Edward, whom she hoped someday would become King of England.

With the king held in the 'protection' of his Yorkist cousins, Margaret's options where limited. However, she did not sit idly by and allow the Yorkists to have it all their own way, and set about planning the 'liberation' of the king. Her first action was to send word to her adherents in the North, the Earl of Northumberland and Lord Clifford (who were, along with Henry Beaufort, Duke of Somerset, united in their wish for revenge against the Yorkists for the death of their respective fathers at St. Albans), plus several other staunch Lancastrians, to make ready for the forthcoming armed struggle. This action was chronicled by William Gregory who wrote:

> 'Then the queen having knowledge of this party while she sent unto the Duke of Somerset, at that time being in Dorsetshire at the castle of Corfe, and for the Earl of Devonshire, and for Alexander Hody, and prayed them to come to her hastily as they might, with their tenants as strong in their harness to war, for the Lord Roos, the

Queen Margaret, wife of Henry VI. In contrast to her weak-minded husband she was a strong-willed and determined woman, who was prepared to fight for the succession to the throne of her son Edward. This put her on a collision course with Richard Duke of York.

Lord Clifford, the Baron of Greystock, the Lord Neville, the Lord Latimer, were waiting upon the Duke of Exeter to meet with her in Hull. And this matter was not tarried but full privily i-wrought; and she sent letters unto all her chief officers that they would do the same, and that they should warn all who servants that loved her or purposed to keep or rejoice their office, to wait upon her at Hull by that day as it appointed by her. All these people gathered and conveyed so privily that they were whole in number of 15,000 ere any man would believe it; in so much if any man said, or told, or talked of such gathering, he should be schende, (disgraced) and some were in great danger, for the common people said by thoo that told the truth, 'Ye talk right ye would it were', and given no credence of their saying. But last the lords proposed to know the truth.' [1]

Hall, in his account, is more vocal, and in his chronicle he tells us a little of what he believed the queen's plans were:

'The Duke of York well knowing, that the queen would spurn and impugne the conclusions agreed and taken in this parliament (the Act of Accord), caused her and her son, to be sent for by the king: but she being a manly woman, wishing to rule and not be ruled, & there to counselled by the Dukes of Exeter and Somerset, not only denied to come, but also assembled together a great army, intending to take the king by fine force, out of the lords hands, and set them to a new school. The protector lying in London, having perfect knowledge of all these doings.' [2]

Margaret's second task (after summoning her allies in the north, writing to them while she was at the port of Hull), was to travel to Wales in person, and to enlist the support of Jasper Tudor, Earl of Pembroke and his father Owen Tudor (Owain Ap Maredudd Ap Tudor), King Henry VI's stepfather – both staunch Lancastrians – against the Yorkists. It is claimed that on her travels to Wales, her small contingent was set upon by men under the command of Thomas, Lord Stanley. However, she and her son managed to escape and complete her journey to Wales. Later, when these plans were completed, she boarded a ship from Wales bound for Scotland. There she would enlist Scottish support and raise a mercenary army which would unite with the Lancastrians gathering in England. Meanwhile, the Yorkists were not unaware of what Margaret, and her Lancastrian followers were plotting, and set about planning their response to Margaret's opening moves, as the following chronicle shows:

'After these things the Duke of York, knowing for certaine that the queen would not be content with the decree of this parliament [appointing him successor to the crown] made speede into Yorkshire to pursue her...

'Likewise the queen, who was resolved in minde to demand her husbande by dint of swoorde, and for that cause had alreadie assembled a puissant armie, against them.' [3]

Autumn passed into winter and the Lancastrian strength grew, their muster being an exceptionally large one: no mean feat when one considers the time of year. It is perhaps testament to the general feeling of resentment towards the Yorkists – regarding the Act of Accord – that so many flocked to the Lancastrian muster point.

In the meanwhile, the Yorkist plans to counteract the Lancastrians were almost complete. The Duke of York (having first made his will) made plans to march north to deal with the Lancastrians in person, an action increasingly necessary, not only to counter the Lancastrians gathering in the North and 'protect the northern fortress', but also to save his Yorkshire tenants. The latter, although they were few in number, and mainly congregated in the South (West Riding) of the County of Yorkshire as previously mentioned, was predominantly a Lancastrian heartland. They were, nevertheless, suffering greatly at the hands of the marauding Lancastrians, in the absence of an effective Yorkist government in the North. Indeed, many of the duke's followers and tenants were forced to join with the Lancastrians at sword point – while the Lancastrians plundered their villages and farmsteads – or face the consequences.

Soldiers sack a town during the Wars of the Roses.

Richard also commissioned his eldest son Edward, Earl of March, with his first independent command, and ordered him to follow in Margaret's footsteps and put down the growing rebellion against the Yorkists in Wales. However, due to the fact that York had so few supporters in the North, Edward was ordered to follow on to Yorkshire, as soon as possible, to assist his father in suppressing the Lancastrians. At the same time the Duke of York gave a commission to the Earl of Warwick to remain in London to 'protect' the king as the following chronicle shows:

> 'The Duke of York protector being at London [Baynard's Castle], assigned the Duke of Norfolk, and the Earl of Warwick his trusted friends, to be about the king, and he with the Earl of Salisbury and the Earl of Rutland, and a convenient number of men, departed out of London, the second of December, and sent to the Earl of March his eldest son to follow him with all his power...' [4]

As preparations were taking place, parliament was called, and Warwick's brother, George Neville, opened the proceedings with a rousing speech comparing the Yorkist's cause to a religious one. The context of his words were not lost on the modern historian P. A. Johnson, who wrote the following regarding them:

> 'When Bishop Neville opened parliament, he chose as his text lines from the prophet Joel; in the circumstances a shrewd choice. The prophet's call was for repentance, self-sacrifice, and unity of purpose in the face of an invading army, the invader from the north...
>
> '...The decision to go north, implicit in Neville's sermon, was not an easy one to take in November. Some at least, thought that Queen Margaret to be in Wales with the Earl of Pembroke, robbed of her cash, but confident of reinforcements. They were wrong, as York and his advisors may have known, but even had she not been in the north there was an urgent need to intervene there as quickly as possible, partly to prevent vital castles being handed over to the Scots or the queen, or both, partly to restore order before the trouble could spill south. This was not just a problem of localised rioting. The Earl of Northumberland was actively constructing an army in Yorkshire, ordering all men aged between sixteen and sixty to enlist to rescue the king...' [5]

Clearly, the Duke of York realised that the heart of the Lancastrian strength lay in the northern counties. He also realised that his arrival in Yorkshire would not be celebrated by the local people, as the author of *An English Chronicle of the reigns of Richard II, Henry IV, V, VI*, implies:

> '...and anon after the said Duke of York, the Earl of Rutland his son, and the Earl of Salisbury, a little before Christmas, with a few persons went in to the north also, for to repress the malaice of the northern men the which loved not the said Duke of York ne the Earl of Salisbury...' [6]

The Duke left London on the 2 December, although some believe he himself did not leave the capital until the 9th, a week later, and made steady progress towards Yorkshire. The date of the duke's departure on the 2nd is mentioned in a number of near contemporary accounts, not least Hall, who claims the following:

> '...and he with the Earls of Salisbury, and Rutland: with a convenient company, departed out of London, the second date of December Northward, and sent to the Earl of March his eldest son to follow him with all his power...' [7]

The encounter at Worksop

The chosen route of the duke and his followers, was initially to travel along the 'Great North Road'. Although the order in which the duke organised his forces is not recorded, he must have travelled in the customary three wards, 'vanguard', 'middle' and 'rearguard'. One must assume, that he expected to find provisions and supplies along the way and, as such, the Yorkists baggage train was quite small.

At the same time as the Duke of York was travelling towards Yorkshire, the Duke of Somerset was also travelling north from his castle at Corfe. Delayed in his arrival at the muster point with the other Lancastrians in Yorkshire, due to the fact that he had previously been in France trying to break the Yorkist hold on the fortress and Port of Calais, he along with the Earl of Devon and several other Lancastrians who were also travelling north clashed with elements of the Yorkist vanguard at or around Worksop. This action was chronicled by William of Worcester, who wrote that the army of the Duke of York:

> '...coming unexpectedly upon the troops of the Duke of Somerset at Worksop, their vanguard (the Yorkists) was destroyed...' [8]

Little is known of this encounter, and the date that it occurred is not recorded. However, it seems unlikely that the Duke of York's entire vanguard was totally destroyed as Worcester implies. The reason for this is that it is doubtful that this was a planned encounter. Indeed, the words of the chronicle indicate that the Yorkist vanguard, or at least elements of it, probably the mounted forerunners, scouts etc, came across the Lancastrians, and not the other way around.

With the Lancastrians having superior numbers, it is probable that the Yorkists came off the worst in the skirmish, although the Yorkist numbers involved would have been very small in the first place. Somerset, thus made aware of the Yorkist advance and conscious that York's army probably outnumbered his own, swiftly ordered his men on towards Pontefract before the main Yorkist army could fall upon him now that his location was known to them.

It is still not clear today which location in Yorkshire the Duke of York was originally heading for. We should recall, that the duke's initial plan – while unaware of the Lancastrian strength – was, as previously mentioned, to travel directly up the Great North Road to Pontefract and confront the Lancastrians. However, due to the fact that Worksop is not located on the Great North

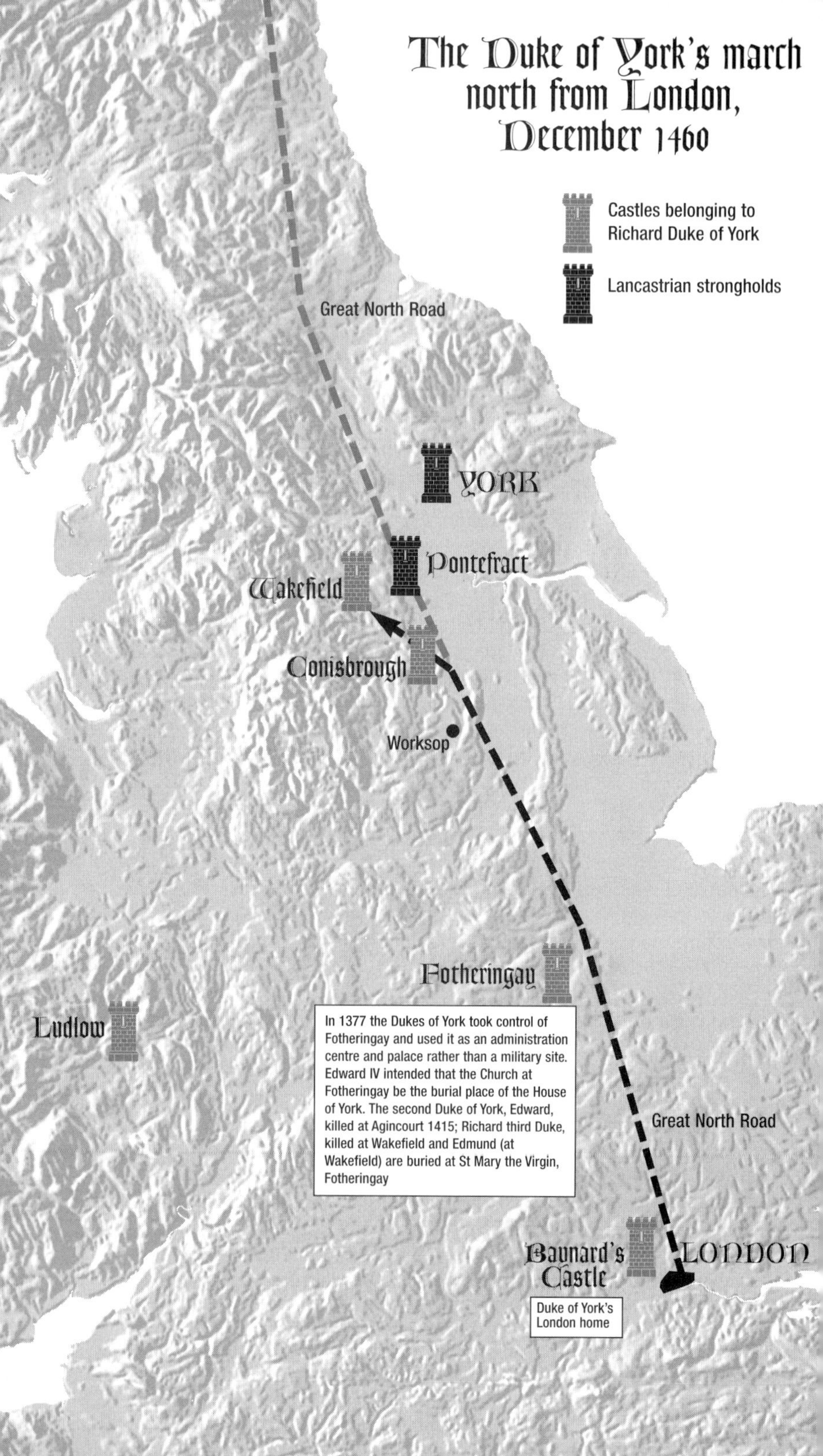

The Duke of York's march north from London, December 1460
Castles belonging to Richard Duke of York
Lancastrian strongholds
Great North Road
YORK
Pontefract
Wakefield
Conisbrough
Worksop
Fotheringay
Ludlow
In 1377 the Dukes of York took control of Fotheringay and used it as an administration centre and palace rather than a military site. Edward IV intended that the Church at Fotheringay be the burial place of the House of York. The second Duke of York, Edward, killed at Agincourt 1415; Richard third Duke, killed at Wakefield and Edmund (at Wakefield) are buried at St Mary the Virgin, Fotheringay
Great North Road
Baynard's Castle
LONDON
Duke of York's London home

Road, something must have occurred to make the Yorkists change direction.

To answer why this may be, I suggest the following. It could be argued that after the artillery had been forced to return to London – due to bad weather, as previously mentioned – and even before the encounter at Worksop, the duke, advised by his many councillors and probably working from more recent 'intelligence', first concluded that the Lancastrians were, in actual fact, in greater numbers than he had originally anticipated. As such, he concluded that the current strength of his army may not have been sufficient to force a siege at Pontefract or face the Lancastrians in open battle.

It was only after concluding this that the Duke and his advisors sought another destination at which to await the arrival of reinforcements, (namely the Earl of March who was in the meantime heading toward Wales with his own command), before travelling to Pontefract to confront the Lancastrians. With this, the choice of leaving the 'Great North Road' and heading towards the duke's castle at Sandal, rather than travelling directly north to Pontefract to confront the enemy head on, was decided upon.

Artillery and the Yorkist march north

There appears to be a lot of confusion over the size of the duke's baggage and artillery train. The author of *An English Chronicle of the reigns of Richard II, Henry IV, V, VI,* page 106 – 107, implies that there was '...a great ordnance of guns and other stuffs of war...', in the duke's retinue as it marched north. By contrast, Goodman, in his work *The Wars of the Roses,* (page 42), claims that the duke left with only a few hundred followers, and Salisbury with less than a hundred, and as such they were forced to recruit on the way. Boardman, in his work, *The Battle of Towton 1461,* (page 26) claims, in regards to the Wakefield campaign, that the artillery was forced to turn back due to bad weather – a view reinforced by the fact that there was no artillery involved in the battle of Wakefield. Whereas, Gillingham, in *The Wars of the Roses,* (page 119) claims that the duke left with a force of 6,000 men. Clearly, there is no continuity regarding the whole issue of York's march north. Even the contemporary and near contemporary chroniclers are at a loss, other than to state that on their march to Wakefield, they met the Lancastrians at Worksop, and that they arrived at Sandal sometime between the 21 and 24 December.

The issue of the ravaging and pillaging of York's properties in Yorkshire (as previously mentioned), most notably by Northumberland and Clifford, certainly had a bearing on York's decision to travel north. However, we should not lose sight of the fact that it was principally the recovery of northern fortresses – such as Pontefract – that was the main reason for the expedition. In regards to this, Ross, in *Edward IV,* (page 29), writes that:

> '...by October the (Yorkist) government had been reduced to issuing hopeful commands to a mixed bag of Lancastrian and Yorkist partisans to expel evildoers from these castles (Pontefract in

> Yorkshire and Penrith in Cumberland), and to call out 'lieges of Yorkshire and adjacent counties to storm the same', (CPR 1452 – 61, 607 – 8, 610 – 11) in case of resistance. But there was little hope of success...'

One could argue that the above quote not only supports the view that the Duke of York was heading north to confront the Lancastrians directly at Pontefract, in order to take possession of the fortress, but also, how the issue of the plundering of York's estates was a secondary consideration. The previous notes regarding artillery also reinforce the view that he was travelling directly to Pontefract, as he would certainly have required it to enforce a siege of the castle.

Artillery was beginning to become prominent around the time of the battles of the Wars of the Roses.

Chapter Three

The Battle of Wakefield

When the Duke of York reached Sandal Castle, 24 December 1460, he found it badly prepared to sustain the army of 5 to 6,000 which he had brought with him from London. The reason for this is not recorded, but one can assume that with a large Lancastrian force only a short distance away at Pontefract, the Yorkist constable of Sandal Castle was unable, (or perhaps unwilling) to travel the manor, collecting food and supplies ready for the arrival of his master. Or that, because the Duke of York had changed his plans so late in the campaign, the keeper of the castle was not given sufficient warning – or not notified at all – as to the duke's intention to come to Sandal. Whatever the reason, that fact remained that the duke found the castle ill-prepared upon his arrival.

The strength of the castle keep and stout walls amounted to a formidable presence within the surrounding countryside, nonetheless, it was a small stronghold when compared to the likes of Dunstanburgh, Ludlow and Pontefract. Consequently, the whole contingent of troops under the duke's command would not have taken up residence within the security of the castle walls. It could only have housed somewhere in the region of 500 to 600, men. Two hundred years later, during the

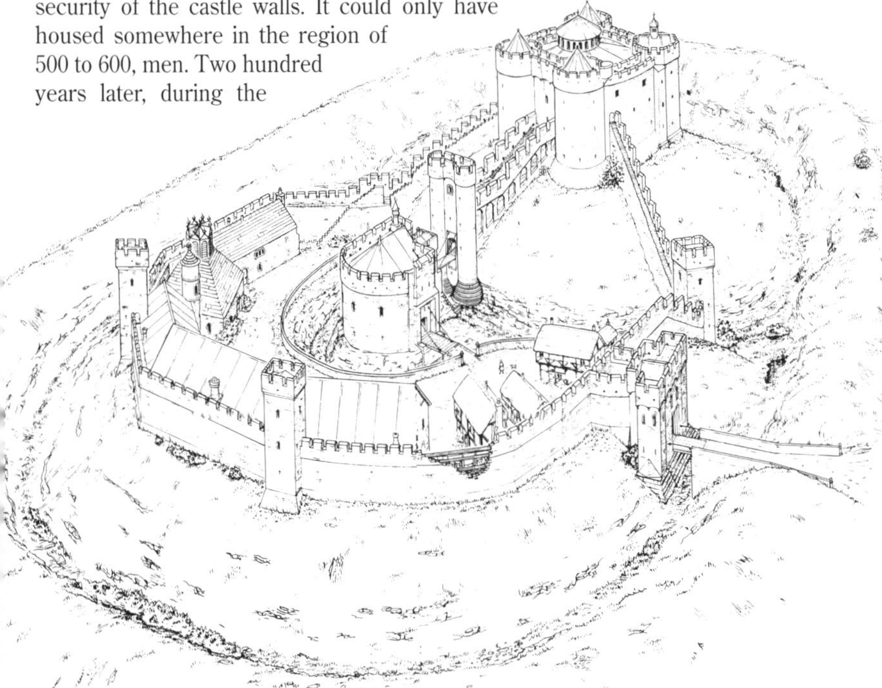

BY COURTESY OF WAKEFIELD HISTORICAL PUBLICATIONS

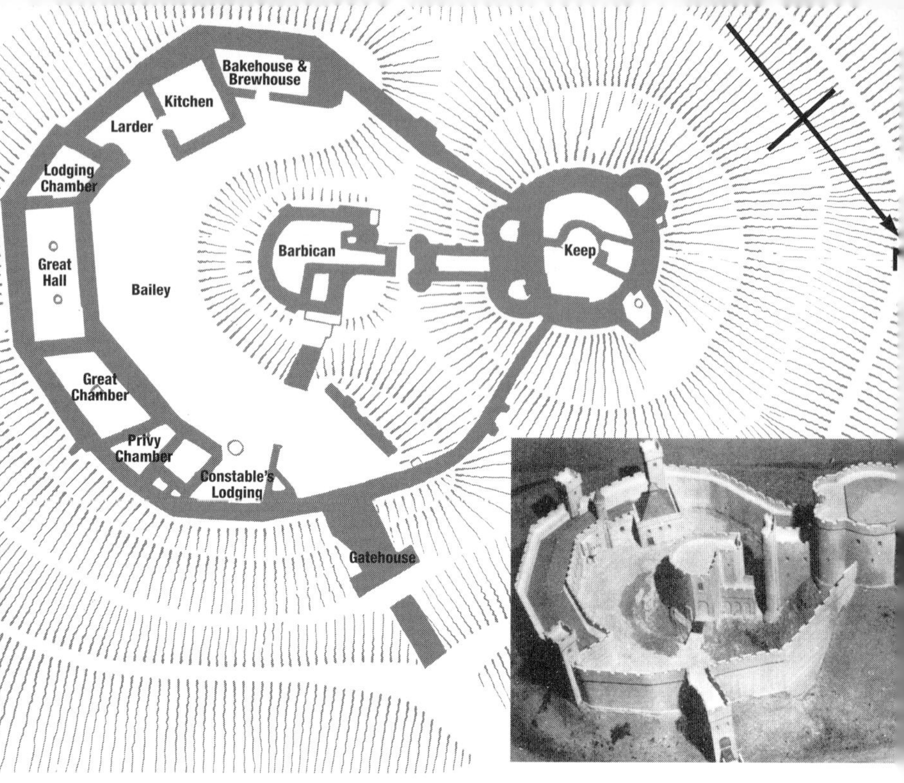

A Plan of Sandal Castle based upon a diagram made in 1893.

Inset: A model of the castle. The fortress was not large enough to hold the entire Yorkist force of 5,000 men in December 1460.

English Civil War, the castle garrison comprised of one hundred men, and that force held out against a sieging Parliamentarian force for a considerable length of time. In fact, the castle was never taken by force of arms and was only surrendered after the garrison obtained favourable terms.

Keeping in mind the size of the castle the Duke's men would have bivouacked in the immediate surrounds of the fortress and, considering that it was the depths of winter, the town of Wakefield would have drawn men to its shelter. What effect this had on the local people is not recorded. However, with food in short supply and the harsh winter weather making living conditions even more difficult to bear than usual, the Yorkist commanders would have encouraged their men to set out on extended foraging duties to provide victuals for the army.

The Lancastrians, ensconced at the much larger Pontefract Castle, were well aware that the Duke of York had arrived in the area, especially as they had encountered portions of the Duke's vanguard at Worksop weeks earlier. Nor would it have taken much deduction to work out that Sandal was the Duke's likely destination as it was his principal stronghold in Yorkshire, his closest other castle being at Conisborough. Constant surveillance of the

Duke's property by Lancastrian scouts would have been prudent and most likely. It must have been a time of great concern for the Duke of York, isolated in his castle and short of both supplies and reinforcements and believing that his enemy faced him in overwhelming numbers. Even his attempts to recruit locally had failed him as the chronicler de Waurin noted:

> '...The Duke of York, who was then staying in Wakefield, hearing that the Queen Margaret was coming with the Duke of Somerset and a big group of armed men in order to fight, was as such concerned for at that time he did not have enough people to resist against such a demonstration of force.
>
> 'He talked with the Earl of Salisbury and all the people on his side to review their situation and tried to get people from everywhere in an attempt to increase their strength and power within the town [castle], but all this did not suffice as at that time [time of invasion] most of the people were out in the fields...'[1]

Therefore, the Yorkists and the Lancastrians, the one side being at Sandal, the other nine miles away at Pontefract, celebrated their Christmas – in the perfect knowledge of each other's presence, and no doubt planning how best to bring about each other's demise.

The Lancastrians spent the next three days gathering their forces. The reason for this delay was probably due to the fact that the Lancastrians were also engaged in scouring the shire looking for provisions and, therefore, it took some time for their commanders to muster their men together to move against the Yorkists at Wakefield.

Meanwhile at Sandal Castle, York also set about gathering his forces, as the following chroniclers noted, Stow commented that:

> 'The duke came to the castle of Sandal besides Wakefield on Christmas Eve, and there began to assemble his tenants and friends. There came to him under the colour of friendship, the Lord Neville, brother of the Earl of Westmoreland, and requested of him a commission for him to raise the people...'[2]

Whereas, the author of *An English Chronicle of the reigns of Richard II, Henry IV, V, VI*, wrote the following:

> 'Then the Lord Neville, brother to the Earl of Westmoreland, under false colour went to the said Duke of York, desiring a commission of him for to raise a people for to chastise the rebels of the county; and the duke it granted...'[3]

Because of the somewhat lengthy processes of recruiting in the fifteenth century it is unlikely that Lord Neville visited the duke on his arrival at Sandal. With the battle only three or four days hence, he could not have raised an army of 8,000 men (which we are told he brought to the field) in such a short space of time. And appear they did on the field of battle at the crucial time. He would have sought and obtained his commission some time earlier. While sending messages to the duke on his travels – and on the Duke of York's arrival at Sandal – he would have informed him of the progress in obtaining recruits.

The march to do battle

Here then was an opportunity to put an end to the Duke of York and his supporters once and for all. The duke was an ever-present threat to the kingship of England; to King Henry VI and a bar to the succession of his issue, and to the House of Lancaster.

It was on the morning of the 28 December that the Lancastrians set out from Pontefract marching the nine miles westward towards the Yorkists gathered in and around Sandal Castle. their route would have taken them along the high ground through the village of Croften, and close to Walton village. The force, believed to be in excess of 15,000 drew near to Sandal, being reasonably hidden from the view of the castle by travelling along the base of the ridge on which Walton village stands.

The order of battle in which the Lancastrians approached Sandal is believed to have been as follows:

> 'Lord Clifford, with his Yorkshire friends, ("the Flower of Craven") led the van, so as to become the right wing in forming the battle, resting on the River Calder. The Dukes of Somerset and Exeter and Earls of Devon and Northumberland were in the centre. The rear, which would form the left wing in wheeling into line, was under the command of the Earl of Wiltshire. Sir Andrew Trollope was the principal military adviser and chief of staff.'[4]

(Referring to Andrew Trollope as 'Sir' at this point, is in fact incorrect, he was not knighted until after the battle of St. Albans the following February).

Edward Hall in his account of the events, gives some clues as to the disposition of the Lancastrian commanders:

> 'The Duke of Somerset and other of the queen's part knowing perfectly that if the duke got the victory, their days were finished, and their livings left bare, like men quickened and exasperate, for the safeguard of their lives and defence of their goods, determined to abide the chance, and to espy their most advantage, and so appointed the Lord Clifford, to lie in the one stole [ambush], and the Earl of Wiltshire in the other, and they themselves kept the main battle...'[5]

As the Lancastrian army drew closer to Sandal Castle, some time on the 28 December they would have been reported on by Yorkist scouts. It caused the Yorkists to retreat towards the safety afforded by Sandal Castle itself. The castle could not hold within its walls the whole of the Yorkist force and those not absent on foraging duties in the surrounding countryside would have taken up a position on the flat ground in front of the castle, north of the fortress, at the southern edge of Wakefield Green.

At this point, it appears that the 'centre' of the Lancastrian army led by Somerset, Northumberland and the others mentioned above, took up a position north of Wakefield Green, but south of the river facing the Yorkists within and around the castle. With the troops from both sides in position, it appears that for the next twenty-four hours the Lancastrians taunted the

Duke of York, trying to draw him from his stronghold as the Lancastrians, had no siege equipment with them. Doubtless, without the experienced personnel to conduct the necessary works required for imposing a siege, they were aware that the longer the Duke of York maintained his position within the castle and immediate surrounds, then the greater the likelihood that he would be reinforced, and as such they were desperate to draw him into battle.

In what form these taunts were is not recorded. However, it appears that they went along the lines that the Duke was acting like a coward, staying behind the walls of the castle and was scared to come out and face a woman – a reference to Queen Margaret. This matter of York being taunted is mentioned not only in the work of Freeman (page 282) and Crowther (page 19), but also less reliably, in the graphic account by Stansfield (pages 29 – 30). Ramsay, in his account, says that it was the fact that the Lancastrians made a 'bold advance' to Wakefield to engage in combat with the Yorkists, which brought the Duke of York from behind the safety of the castle walls.

Although it is clear that the queen was not present at Wakefield at this time, there is no reason to believe that the Duke of York was aware of that fact. Indeed, as far as he was concerned, he most likely thought she was. We will never be sure of what intelligence the duke had in terms of who was present within the Lancastrian ranks.

However, these taunts seem to have gnawed at the Duke of York's honour, for it appears he was keen to oblige the Lancastrians and issue forth and offer battle. It is mentioned by more than one chronicler (and more modern day historians as well) that there was a meeting held in one of the great chambers at Sandal Castle to discuss this, which, it is also said, the Duke of York, his son, the Earl of Rutland, the Earl of Salisbury, Sir David Hall and several other Yorkist commanders were present.

Richard Duke of York. Relatively secure behind Sandal Castle walls Richard had to be tempted to come out and give fight. The Lancastrians used taunts and insults to lure the Duke of York into the open ground between Sandal and Wakefield.

One historian puts the following words into the mouths of the participants:

> '...and although, Sir Davy Hall, his old servant and chief counseillor, advised him to keep his castle and to defend the same with his small number till his son the Earl of March were come with his power of Marchmen and Welsh soldiers; yet he would not be counselled, but in a great fury said, "Ah' Davy, Ah' Davy, hast thou loved me so long, and now wouldst have me dishonoured?
>
> "'Thou never saw me keep fortress when I was Regent of Normandy, when the Dauphin himself, with his puissance came

to besiege me, but like a man, and not like a bird included in a cage, I issued and fought with my enemies, to their loss ever (I thank God) and to my honour. If I have not kept my self within walls for fear of a great and strong prince, nor hid my face from any man living, wouldst thou that I, for dread of a scolding woman, whose weapon is only her tongue, and her nails, should incarcerate myself, and shut my gates? Then all men might of me wonder and all creatures may of me report dishonour, that a woman hath made me d-astard, whom no man ever to this day could yet prove a coward: And surely my mind is rather to die with honour, than to live with shame; for of honour cometh fame, and of dishonour riseth infamy. Their great number shall not appal my spirits, but encourage them; for surely I think that I have there as many friends as enemies, which at joining, will either fly or take my part. Therefore advance my banner, in the name of God and St. George, for surely I will fight with them, though I should fight alone."

'The Earl of Salisbury and other of his friends, seeing his courage, resolved themselves to his opinion, and ordered their men, and set them forth in warlike fashion...'[6]

This was despite the advice of his followers, and as Stow chronicled:

'The duke having with him some fully 5,000. Men contrary to the mind of his faithful friends would needs issue forth to fight with his enemies.'[7]

Thus, it appears that the Duke, viewing the Lancastrian numbers from the castle, perceived that the Lancastrians appeared not to be as numerous as had first thought and, consequently, decided to do battle with them. However, before the Duke could leave the castle it appears that a separate event occurred, in that one of the many foraging parties sent out by the Yorkists chose that moment to return to the castle. It became embroiled in a running fight with combat with the Lancastrians to the north of Wakefield Green. Leadman mentions this as follows:

'Vexed at want of success on the part of his foragers, and hunger staring him in the face, York decided to give battle to the pursuers. This step was taken against the advice of Sir David Hall, who strongly urged him to await help from the Earl of March.'[8]

With this, the duke '...trusting to his owne knowledge in warefare...' as Polydore Vergil put it, sallied forth from the castle down onto Wakefield Green, towards the waiting Lancastrians. This initial move is well chronicled as follows:

'...trusting to his owne knowledge in warfare, and the valience of his soldiers, yssued out of his campe against his enemyes in good array.'[9]

Edward Hall, in his account is more vocal and wrote the following:

'The Earl of Salisbury and other of his friends, seeing his courage, resolved themselves to his opinion, and ordered their men, and set them forth in warlike fashion...

'...The Duke of York with his people, descended down the hill in

Sandal Castle in the 16th Century.

BARNSLEY LIBRARIES, ARCHIVES & LOCAL STUDIES DEPARTMENT

> good order and array and was suffered to pass forward, toward the main battle: but when he was in the plain ground between his castle and the town of Wakefield...'[10]

These accounts give a good indication of where the battle took place, '...in the plain field between his castle and the town of Wakefield...', or, as it is known today, Wakefield Green. Thus the two sides were joined in battle. Unfortunately, there is no indication as to what time during the day the battle began, although it was probably early in the afternoon between midday and 2 o'clock.

Battle commences and a trap is sprung

Leading up to the confrontation at Wakefield, Lord Neville had been in constant communication with the duke, consequently his arrival on the field of battle would not have been unexpected by Richard. With Neville's 8,000 men, added to the Duke of York's 5,000, then the odds of 13,000 Yorkists against the Lancastrian 15,000 – 18,000 would have appeared decidedly more attractive to the duke. This would certainly have influenced his decision to leave the safety of the castle and attack the Lancastrians. This could be what is meant by de Waurin when he writes:

> '...accompanied by other warriors, informed the Duke of York, without introducing themselves, that they were coming to rescue him, which made the duke so joyful that he went outside the town [castle] to fight his enemies.'[11]

We should also bear in mind the words of Hall, who suggested that the duke claimed:

> 'Their great number shall not appal my spirits, but encourage them; for surely I think that I have there as many friends as enemies, which at joining, will either fly or take my part. Therefore advance my banner, in the name of God and St. George, for surely I will fight with them, though I should fight alone'...'[12]

It is likely that Lord Neville approached the battlefield from the north – from the direction of Wakefield bridge. His appearance came just as the Lancastrians were attacking the Yorkist foraging party and the Duke of York, believing that he had the opportunity to catch the Lancastrians in a pincer movement, made his move from the castle.

The Yorkists no doubt paraded under the banners of the Duke of York, bearing the usual device of the Plantagenet family, which in the Duke of York's case, was a falcon volant Argent, with a fetterlock. In this battle however, the falcon had its wing extended as if to attempt to open the lock, in reference it is said, by the historian Markham, to York's claim to the throne, the throne being represented by the lock itself.

Many of the Duke's men would have been mounted, and they would have issued forth from the castle and surrounding camp, before forming up en masse. With the Duke of York at the head and in response to his cry and example the Yorkists charged down hill directly at the Lancastrian line, withstanding an arrow storm let loose, as they thundered across the ground between them. It is likely that the two sides hit full on in a line running east from the location of where 'Portbello House' once stood, thus explaining why remnants of the battle were found at that point in later years.

Unwittingly, in this event, the Duke had been drawn into a trap. He charged deep into the ranks of the enemy, joining up with the survivors of the foraging party and pushing the front of the Lancastrians back towards the River Calder. It supports the account that the Lancastrians were standing on the ground – at the start of the battle – a little to the south of the location which is today called the 'Fall Ings', an area which was given that name due to the numbers of combatants who fell there during the fighting.

Initially the Yorkists, many of whom were mounted, came off the better against their foes, who were predominantly on foot. During this first contact the Lancastrians reeled under the initial shock of the impact of the ferocious charge. They gave up some ground as they were pushed back towards Wakefield, along the route they had advanced to come to blows with the Yorkists. Whether this giving up of ground was a deliberate ploy by the Lancastrians to draw the Yorkists further away from the sanctuary of the

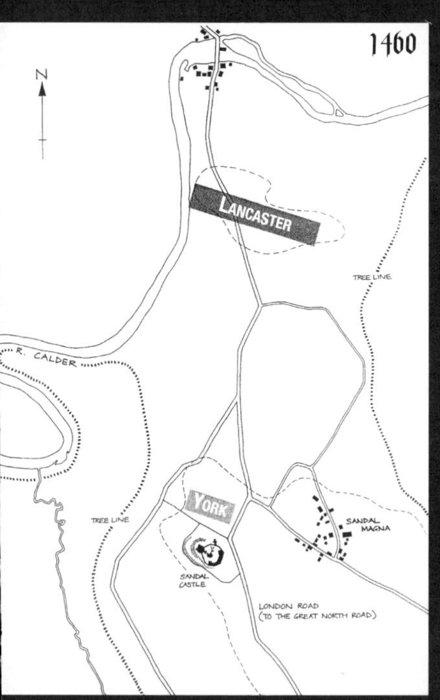

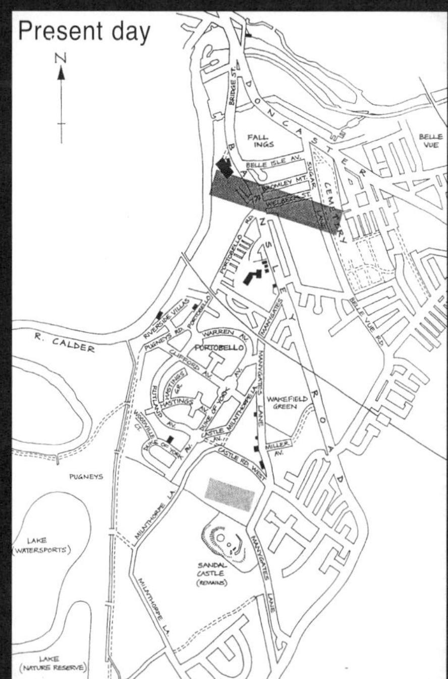

Opening positions of the battle, midday, 30 December, 1460

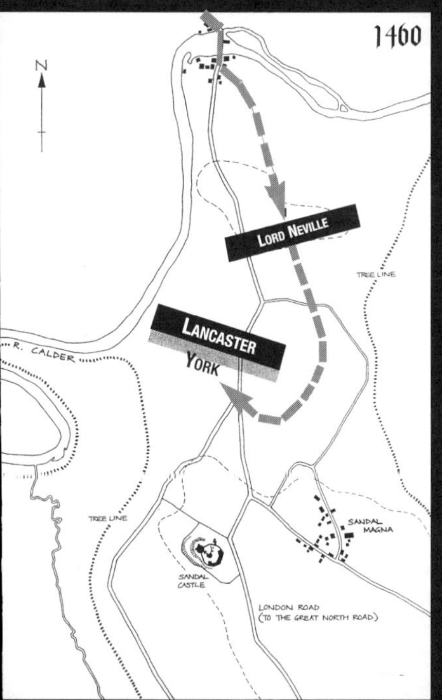

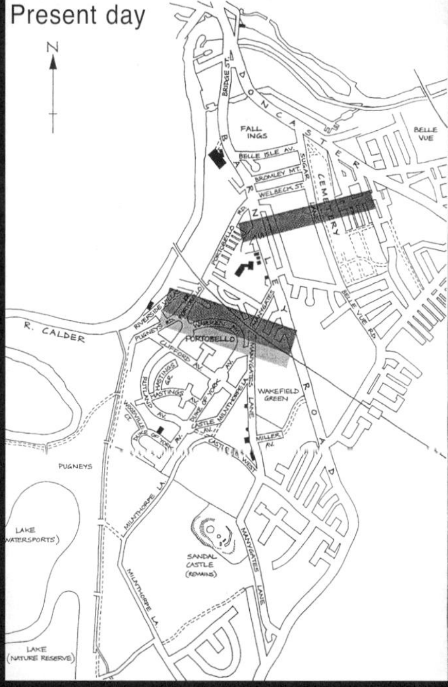

Lord Neville's 8,000 men are observed by The Duke of York approaching the Lancastrians from the rear. Believing that he had the advantage the Duke gave the order to charge – however, Neville had changed sides and the Yorkists were doomed.

Richard Duke of York headed the charge from Sandal Castle at the massed ranks of Lancastrians, believing that Lord Neville was about to attack the enemy from the rear. BY COURTESY OF WAKEFIELD HISTORICAL PUBLICATIONS

castle is not clear. These opening moves and the subsequent encircling manoeuvre is well documented by the chroniclers. Polydore Vergil wrote:

> 'At the beginning the fight was mightily mainteyned mutually, while that a great part of them who were in the front battaile being killed, the Duke of Yorkes small number was environd [surrounded] of the multitude.'[13]

And Hall the following:

> '...but when he was in the plain ground between his castle and the town of Wakefield, he was environed on every side, like a fish in a net, or a deer in a buck-stall...'[14]

It is said that the troops employed to carry out these Lancastrian flanking attacks were lightly armoured infantry or light cavalry, known as 'prickers'. This was a name given to them, in reference to the fifteen-foot lances that they carried, which amongst other uses, were employed to discourage deserters from leaving the ranks of the army whilst they were travelling on their campaigns. Thus lightly armed it allowed them to quickly traverse the distance from the rear of the Lancastrian ranks and encircle the Yorkists.

The Yorkists, now surrounded on every side, attempted a fighting retreat towards the castle. The battle flowed back along the Wakefield to Sandal road – or as it was later called, 'Cock and Bottle Lane'.

Alas, for the Duke of York, fate was to strike a final deadly blow. Already faced with the overwhelming odds presented by the entire Lancastrian army – the duke now had to contend with treachery as well. Lord Neville who entered the field at that point with some 8,000 troops, originally commissioned to come to the Duke of York's aid, declared for the Lancastrians and with this act sealed the fate of the Yorkist army. It was only when the Duke of York had crossed Wakefield Green, and reached the fray, did he realise that Lord Neville – who, he originally thought had arrived in 'the nick of time' to assist him – was actually against him. Thus fooled and outmanoeuvred, the fate of the Duke and his small army of faithful followers, was sealed.

This change of sides was noted by the author of *An English Chronicle of the reigns of Richard II, Henry IV, V, VI,* who wrote:

> 'Then the Lord Neville, brother to the Earl of Westmoreland, under false colour...
>
> '...raised a number of 8,000 men, and brought them to the lords of the country; that is to say, the Earl of Northumberland, Lord Clifford, and Duke of Somerset, that were adversaries and enemies to Duke Richard.'[15]

There was to be no escape. All that was left for the adherents to the banner of York was to die bravely. Stansfield in his colourful account of the battle, takes up the story:

> 'The engagement now became wider and fiercer, and the carnage was frightful. If the Lancastrians were weak in archers, they were strong in swordsmen, who now wielded their arms with deadly effect at such close quarters. The duke's handful of troops fought with surpassing courage against the vastly superior forces of the enemy, and for a time the fortunes of the day wavered in the balance...
>
> '...the battle soon began to assume an unfavourable aspect for the Yorkists. Still the brave army of Richard fought on gallantly against overpowering odds. Wherever his presence was most needed, there was Richard in the thickest of the fight, animating his men by his dauntless bearing, and urging them on by his ringing war cry. His matchless valour was conspicuous on all sides, and he inspired his followers with a spirit of indomitable bravery almost equal to his own.
>
> 'The uproar of the battle swelled mightier and mightier: the shock of steed, the clash of steel, the hiss of arrows, the shouts of the victors, and the cries of the wounded, all told that the crisis of the battle was come. Father fought against son, brother against brother, and kith against kin; and the fight was so deadly, very little quarter was given on either side. More cavalry and infantry arrived on the scene, fresh and panting for the fray, and shouting "Exeter to the onslaught!"'
>
> '...though his warrior yeoman were thrown into disorder, still the

untiring might of Richard's arm defied for a time the wave upon wave of troops that attacked his doomed army; but as well attempt to stem the tide of ocean as for that scattered army to resist the overwhelming torrent of foes that rushed upon them...'[16]

The Duke of York, sensing that the end was near, thought of the safety of his son the Earl of Rutland. The young lad had become separated from his father's force. The decision was made by the earl's tutor Sir Robert Aspall, who accompanied him, to escape the slaughter.

The Duke of York died on the field of battle with his back to a clump of three willow trees, for protection, facing his enemies. Markham gives the following account:

'The Duke of York fell fighting to the last. Camden says that there was a small space, hedged round, enclosing a stone cross on the spot where the duke fell; and Gibson adds that there, before the civil war between Charles I. and his parliament, the owners were obliged, by

Cut off from Sandal Castle Richard Duke of York makes his last stand at the willow trees

Pour bon amour

Ring found on the spot where Richard made his last stand. The words* Pour bon amour *(meaning either 'for good love' or 'in true love') were engraved on the inside and Christ, the Virgin Mary and two other saints on the outside. The ring was last seen in the nineteenth century. Its whereabouts are no longer known.

tenure, to keep the hedge. A very ancient willow long marked the spot but it has been cut down within the last few years. (Hutton in his own work says, "The spot was about 400 yards from the Castle, close to the old road from Barnsley to Wakefield," now called, from the sign of the public house "Cock and Bottle Lane". The public house is no longer in existence, but its location can be found on the Ordinance Survey map of the 1850s). On the spot where the duke and his faithful friends made their last stand an antique ring was found. Within it was engraved the

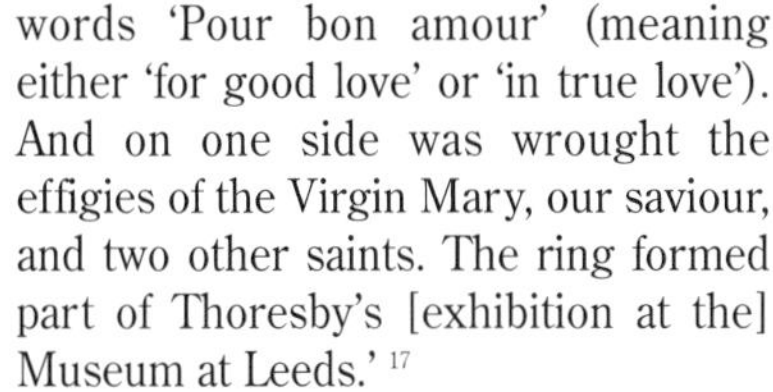

words 'Pour bon amour' (meaning either 'for good love' or 'in true love'). And on one side was wrought the effigies of the Virgin Mary, our saviour, and two other saints. The ring formed part of Thoresby's [exhibition at the] Museum at Leeds.' [17]

The location of the ring today is unknown.

Concerning the exact spot of the duke's last stand, Tyas writing his account in 1854, makes reference to a Mr Norisson Scatcherd who remarked:

'This spot on the right (travelling in the direction of Sandal from Wakefield) of the lane or the old road leading from Wakefield to the Three Houses (a public house) in Sandal, and which was once the London road, is a triangular piece of ground, with a fence about it, which the tenant of the place is bound, by his lease, to maintain. When I saw it, many years ago, some very old trees were growing in the fence, and vestiges of others, still older, were perceptible...'[18]

In pin-pointing this spot, Brooke who visited and wrote about the battlefield of Wakefield in 1852, mentions the site of the Duke's demise as follows:

'On the right hand side of the road

leading from Wakefield to Barnsley, which passes the castle, and is called Sandal Castle Lane, [previously Cock and Bottle Lane and today 1995, Manygates Lane], is a small field or close, or rather a triangle form, which is said to be the spot where the Duke of York fell.

'It will scarcely admit of any doubt, that this is the identical place which is mentioned in the addition to Camden's *Britannia*, although there is no vestige of the cross now left. The small field or close may easily be distinguished: it lies about a mile from Wakefield Bridge; and at a very trifling distance beyond the toll-bar, a little well (which is clearly marked on both the 1850's and the 1914 Ordinance Survey map), will be remarked, in the hedge, on the right side of the old road to Barnsley; and about midway between the toll-bar and the well, the small field or close presents itself to view. It is remarkable for having two very old willows growing in the hedge adjoining the road; and more of them were not very long ago growing there. A small compartment of the field was, within the recollection of the recent vicar of Sandal, fenced off from the remainder of it, and planted with red and white roses, which must naturally be supposed to have done to commemorate the battle, or the death of the Duke of York.'[19]

The actual circumstances of the death of York, as previously stated, are not recorded, although the story of his 'last stand', with his back to a clump of willow trees, seems to have survived the test of time. Some historians say that he refused 'quarter' preferring death before such a dishonour. Stanfield picked up on this point in his own account as follows:

'At the foot of the steep road which winds from the castle to the lower ground stood at that time some huge trees, and it was with his back to these trees that Richard, with his decimated ranks of gallant soldiers, made his last stand. His rear protected by these gigantic trunks, his front entrenched behind the heaps of the slain, for round this spot had waged the brunt of the battle and the deadliest of the fight, Richard had never before in all his former wars surpassed himself as in this, his last fight; and here, with irresistible valour and with sublime despair, he still fought on.

'The fury of the conflict and the pressure of the excited rear ranks impelled the Lancastrians on, and at length Richard's followers were forced back, and he himself was unhorsed, wounded and beaten to his knees. Many wished to spare him, and were reluctant to strike, but yield he would not! Amidst the din of battle and the victorious cries of the victors were heard loud shouts of 'yield!, yield thee!'. Some of Richard's brave soldiers strove to cover his body, but numbers rushed on and swept the gallant defenders away, and a hundred blows rained down on the duke's armour, and he at last fell, still grasping his sword in his iron hand.' [20]

York's death, in sight of Sandal Castle, brought about the end of the battle and the beginning of the Yorkist rout. In all, other than the majority of the Yorkist commanders present on the field of battle, there were slain some

Detail of the figure of Richard Duke of York from the Victorian monument. The carving was copied from an original statue (right) which once adorned the Welsh bridge at Shrewsbury, but is now in the Market Hall. GW

2,000 – 2,500 Yorkist troops.

The duration of the battle in which this slaughter took place, is mentioned by the chroniclers to have lasted under an hour. The subsequent pursuit of the Yorkists in the rout may have lasted well into the evening, certainly for several more hours. In most of the battles of the Wars of the Roses, the heaviest casualties occurred during the rout. There is no reason to believe that this was not the case at Wakefield. Sufficient numbers of them may have tried to find sanctuary by fleeing towards the town of Wakefield. During this portion of the rout (towards Wakefield) many of the Yorkists, hotly pursued by the Lancastrians, must have been killed before actually crossing the river.

This could be why that area of Wakefield, acquired the name it still retains today, 'Fall Ings' – due to the numbers who fell there. This being the case it would also account for why portions of the Lancastrian army – namely Lord Clifford and his men – were present at that point

As to the taking of the castle itself, Stanfield in his account of the battle, makes the comment:

> 'The castle having been left entirely unguarded was taken early in the day by a party belonging to Lord Wiltshire's force...'[21]

It would be a fair assumption to say, that the Lancastrian capture of the castle was achieved only after the defeat of the Yorkists on the field of battle. It is likely that any Yorkists remaining in the castle as the rout began, realised that the day was lost as they watched the Yorkist defeat occur before them from the vantage point afforded by the walls of the castle. Thus, being aware of what had transpired, and equally, being aware of what treatment would probably befall them should they be captured, they probably took the opportunity to leave the fortress – and the vicinity – before the Lancastrians had time to turn their thoughts to occupying the castle.

The death of Richard's son, the Earl of Rutland

At a point close to the end of the battle, there occurred – as Brooke would later describe in his paper on the battle of Wakefield – an act of, '...shocking wickedness and barbarity...'. He went further to say:

> '...Edmund Plantagenet, Earl of Rutland, a son of the Duke of York, a boy, only twelve years old, [*sic*] was captured when flying with his Tutor from the field of battle, and was put to death near Wakefield Bridge, by Lord Clifford: a murder which obtained for him during the very short remainder of his life, the epithet of 'The Butcher'...'[22]

Brooke was obviously referring in his writings to the works of Leland and Hall, where the latter chronicles Rutland's death as follows:

> 'While this battle was in fighting, a priest called Sir Robert Aspall, chaplain and schoolmaster to the young Earl of Rutland second son to the above named Duke of York, scarce of the age of twelve years, [*sic*] a fair gentleman and a maidenlike person, perceiving that flight was more safeguard than tarrying, both for him and his master, secretly conveyed the earl out of the field, by the Lord Clifford's band towards the town, but ere he could enter into a house, he was by the said Lord Clifford spied, followed, and taken, and by reason of his appearance, demanded what he was.
>
> 'The young gentleman, dismayed, had not a word to speak, but kneeled on his knees imploring mercy, and desiring grace, both with holding up his hands and making dolorous countenance, for his

Richard's son, the seventeen years old Earl of Rutland, was caught in the vicinity of Wakefield bridge by the Lancastrians. Lord Clifford, upon learning who he was, stabbed him to death in vengeful rage. It was a merciless atrocity that would be repaid three months later. GW

speech was gone for fear. "Save him", said his chaplain, "for he is a prince's son, and eradventure may do you good hereafter".

'With that word, the Lord Clifford marked him and said: "By God's blood, thy father slew mine, and so I will do thee and all thy kin", and with that word, struck the earl to the heart with his dagger, and bade his chaplain bear the earl's mother and brother word of what he had done, and said. In this act the Lord Clifford was labelled a tyrant, and no gentleman; for the property of the lion, which is furious and unreasonable beast, is to be cruel to them that withstand him, and gentle to such as prostrate or humiliate themselves before him.

'Yet this cruel Clifford and deadly Bloodsucker not content with this homicide, or child-killing...'[23]

Worcester in his account of the battle only briefly mentions Rutland's demise as follows:

'...After the battle, Lord Clifford slew the young Earl of Rutland, the son of the Duke of York, as he was fleeing across the Bridge at Wakefield...'[24]

As to Rutland being only a boy of twelve – thus compounding this 'murderous act' – this is, in fact, in error, for William of Worcester chronicles the birth of all of the Duke of York's children as follows:

Anna Countess of Exeter born at Fotheringhay Monday 10 August 1439.
Henry born at Hatfield Friday 10 February 1441.
Edward Earl of March born at Rouen Saturday 28 April 1442.
Edmund Earl of Rutland born at Rouen Friday 17 May 1443.
Elizabeth born at Rouen Saturday 22 April 1444.
Margaret born at Fotheringhay Tuesday 3 May 1446.
William born at Fotheringhay Friday 7 July 1447.
John born at Neyte Thursday 7 November 1448.
George Duke of Clarence born in Ireland Tuesday 21 October 1449.
Thomas born 1450.
Richard Duke of Gloucester born at Fotheringhay Monday 2 October 1452.
Ursula born at Fotheringhay Sunday 20 July 1455.[25]

Quite obviously the Earl of Rutland was 17 years of age in 1460.

It is likely, that the young earl and his tutor were amongst a number of Yorkists who tried to escape across the river using the bridge. As to his fleeing the field – it is said that the young Rutland was well versed in the use of arms. In fact, William Gregory, (page 208) writes that Rutland – when it comes to use of arms – was 'One of the best disposed Lords in this land...', and as such it is likely that he fought his way to that location during the rout, and was at that point captured as previously described.

It is not to be doubted that it was at Clifford's own hand that the young Earl of Rutland met his death. It is said of Clifford '...the sight of any of the house of York, was as a fury to torment his soul...' He certainly had the motive, his own father having been killed five years previously at the battle of St. Albans at the hands of the Yorkists. The fate of the earl's tutor – Sir Robert Aspall – is not recorded.

Many believed that the teenager was captured on Wakefield Bridge itself – while trying to gain sanctuary in the chapel that was built upon it. The rebuilt chapel and bridge exist to this day. Leland, however, who visited the field of battle in 1544 wrote that Rutland was murdered:

'...a little above the barres, beyond the Bridge going up into the Town of Wakefield that standith full fairely upon the clyving ground...'

He also stated that:

'The commune saying is there, that the Erle wold have taken ther

> a poore Woman's House for socour, and she for fere shet the Dore and strait the Erle was killid. The Lord Clifford for killing of Men at this Batail was caullid the Boucher...'[26]

For this, and other infamous 'deeds', he is also credited with the name 'Black Faced' and 'Black Hearted Clifford'.

Leland, also makes reference to a cross later being erected to mark the spot of Rutland's demise:

> 'At this place is set up a crosse in rei memoriam...'

It is not certain whether he was referring to the cross erected to mark the location of the Duke of York's death, adjacent to Wakefield Green or, if he was referring to a separate one to mark the spot where his son Rutland is said to have been killed. If the latter is the case, then, unfortunately the exact location of this cross is not known and it certainly did not survive the test of time – and endure to later years for modern day historians to discover.

However, Dr John Walker, who wrote a paper on the history of Wakefield including the bridge and chapel, remarked that:

> 'A cross existed at the bottom of Kirkgate, not far from the bridge, long before the battle of Wakefield, for in the will of Joan de Thorp, dated 12th April 1420, it is thus mentioned.
>
> 'I leave to the repair of the road between the bridge and the high

The mediaeval houses that once stood at the north side of the bridge in Wakefield, known as Six Chimneys, where it has been suggested that Edmund, Earl of Rutland, may have been caught.

cross at the end of Kirkgate, 3s. 4d.'

This shows that a cross did exist some distance from the bridge and it was probably near to 'the barres' or gate at the end of Kirkgate. This cross may have been repaired or even rebuilt after the battle; in Dr Johnston's notes it is stated that the cross was erected after the battle, that 'it was taken away about 25 years ago, and set up in the Monday Market-place, but was pulled down and defaced in the (civil) wars'...' [27]

Concerning the actual location of young Rutland's death, there is sufficient information to suggest that the earl and his tutor – who was more likely to be his tutor in arms rather than his tutor in spiritual matters – were captured at some point beyond the bridge; indeed Barrett, in his account of the battle goes further to say:

> 'The "Six Chimney's" – an alternative site for the death of the Earl of Rutland. The 'Kirkgate site' was formerly pointed out, as close to an ancient six gabled house, with three gables in front and three behind. It's location is, however, near the bottom of Kirkgate just where Park Street joins it – a little above where the train station stands today...
>
> '...near that building called 'Six Chimney's' in Kirkgate Wakefield, is locally supposed to mark the site of Rutland's death...
>
> 'The 'Six Chimneys' itself, however, stands where it did on the day of the fight, and is the only contemporary building remaining in the city.[28]

As to the building itself, in 1941, while the owner and Wakefield Council, who had made an offer to take ownership of the building, were in dispute, the owner feeling that the council was not offering enough money for the building, the building simply collapsed, due to the alterations which had been made to it over the years. After this, the council promptly withdrew their offer and the owner was left to fund the clearance of the site unaided.

The fate of the Earl of Salisbury

Stanfield, who wrote about the battle of Wakefield in a paper read before the Wakefield Photographic Society in 1891, claimed that:

> 'Bonfires were lighted after the battle, and by the fierce glare of these the conquerors buried the bodies of the slain in the grounds of the castle and on the field of battle. A letter written at the time by a son who visited the bloody field in search of the dead body of his father says that, "At midnight the kindly snow fell like a mantle on the dead, and covered the rueful faces staring so fiercely up to heaven"...'[29]

It was after the battle and during this time, it is said, that the Earl of Salisbury, who had escaped from the carnage on the battlefield, was captured by an unnamed servant of Andrew Trollope.

The following day the luckless earl, along with other captured Yorkist leaders, Sir Ralph Stanley, Walter Limbrick, John Harrow and Captain Hanson, were taken to Pontefract Castle. It is generally agreed that the

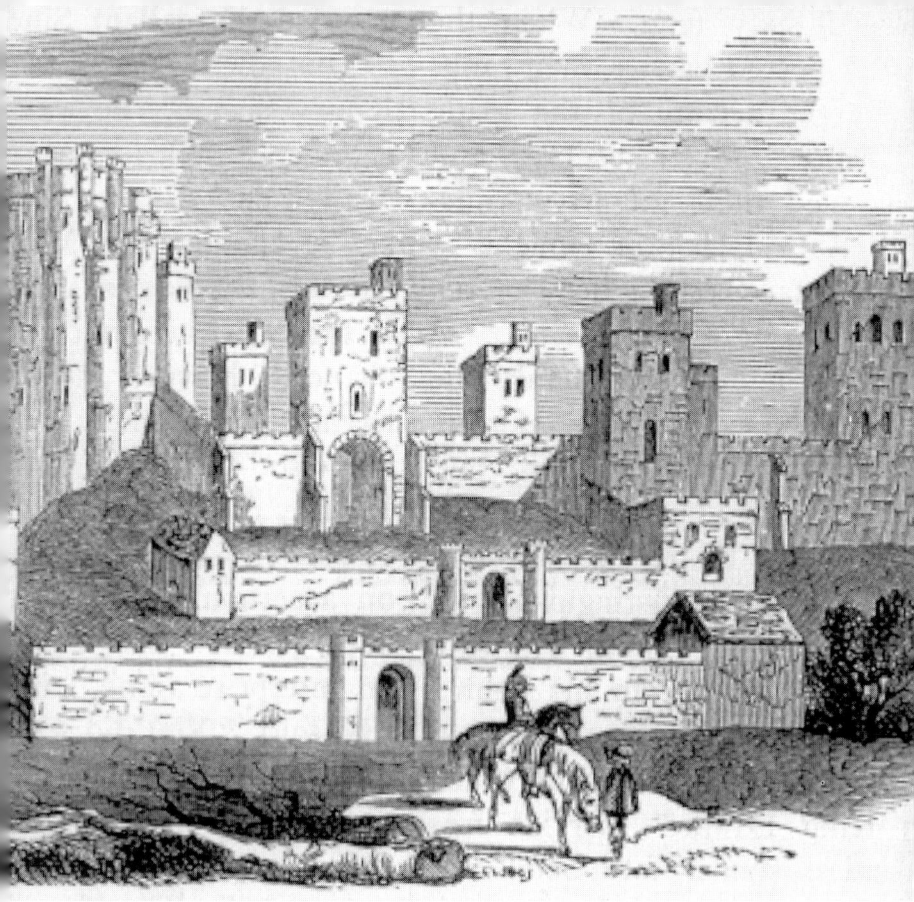

Pontefract Castle, where captives of the Battle of Wakefield were taken along with the bodies of Richard and his son, the Earl of Rutland. There the corpses were mutilated, by decapitation, and the prisoners were also beheaded.

Lancastrians planned to spare the Earl of Salisbury's life in return for a large ransom. However, as William of Worcester went on to chronicle, the Earl of Salisbury and the other prisoners were:

> '... on the morrow beheaded by the Bastard of Exeter at Pontefract.'[30]

Other chroniclers – for example Stow – stated:

> 'The Earl of Salisbury had the grant of his life for a great ransom, but that the common people at Pontefract, who loved him not, took him out of the castle by violence and smote off his head...'[31]

The reason for the earl's unpopularity with the common people who 'loved him not', was due to the fact that Salisbury was the official receiver of those parts. It was in this capacity that, in the years before the battle, he had become unpopular with the local people whilst carrying out his official receiver duties.

The author of *An English Chronicle of the reigns of Richard II, Henry IV, V, VI*, stated:

> 'The Earl of Salisbury was taken alive, and led by the said Duke of Somerset to the castle of Pomfret, and for a great sum of money that he should have paid for grant of his life. But the common people of the county which loved him not, took him from the castle by violence and smote off his head.'[32]

So was it the Bastard of Exeter, illegitimate son of Sir Henry Holland, Duke of Exeter, or the citizens of Pontefract who dragged the Earl of Salisbury to his death? Likely the mob was organised by him.

Certainly, the Earl of Salisbury's son and heir, the Earl of Warwick, believed that Holland the Bastard of Exeter had been actively involved. Less than three months after Salisbury's death, Warwick, then marching with the Yorkist army towards Towton, captured Holland at Coventry, and had him summarily executed in a similar fashion to that of his father.

However, Salisbury's widow implicated another, a certain John Sharp, gent of Pontefract, as her husband's executioner rather than the 'Bastard of Exeter'. Yet another account has the Duchess of Salisbury blaming nine obscure men, aided by retainers of Sir Ralph Percy, for her husband's death. Likely the truth of the matter was, that all those identified had a part to play.

The Lancastrians return to the City of York

After the battlefield was cleared by the victors of the 'debris of battle', and, the salvaging of weapons, armour and personal items, the various Lancastrian nobles present on the field – many of whom were no doubt still 'drunk' with their victory – had knighted a number of their followers. This would have followed the sacking of Sandal Castle, although there must have been precious little to pillage. The victorious Lancastrian army returned to Pontefract Castle, from where, the decision was made to return to York.

During this stage of the campaign, a grizzly act was perpetrated on the dead bodies of the Yorkist commanders. These acts of senseless barbarity, even in that age of ruthless deeds, were deemed excessive, and chronicled by Hall as follows:

> 'Yet this cruel Clifford and deadly Bloodsucker not content with this homicide, or child-killing came to the place where the dead corpse of the Duke of York lay, and caused his head to be stricken off, and set upon it a crown of paper, and so fixed it on a pole...'[33]

With this, the Lancastrians set off towards York, intent on reuniting with Queen Margaret of Anjou, who had, throughout the Wakefield campaign, remained in Scotland gathering support and raising an army of mercenaries. Whether the Duke of Somerset sent a message to Margaret, informing her of their victory and advising her of the meeting place, or whether the rendezvous was preordained, we will never know, in either case the Lancastrians began their journey back to York. It has been claimed by some historians that Margaret was present at, or near to, Wakefield at the time of

Sweet smell of victory! Queen Margaret prepares Richard's head (transported from Pontefract along with the other Yorkists' heads) for the adornment of Micklegate Bar, York. It must have appeared to the Lancastrians that the struggle for domination had finally ended in their favour.

the battle. Hall recorded that Clifford went to the queen with the severed head of York:

'...and presented it to the queen, not lying far from the field, in great despite, and much derision, saying: 'Madam, your war is done, here is your king's ransom', at which present, was much joy, and great rejoicing, but many laughed then that sore lamented after-as the queen herself, and her son. And many were glad then of other men's deaths, not knowing that their own was near at hand-as the Lord Clifford, and other...'[34]

And Stow claims:

'...and presented it to the queen, not lying far from the field. The duke's head with the Earl of Salisbury were set upon a gate of York.' [35]

It is far more likely that the presenting of the heads to Margaret occurred at York. It is not to be doubted that the severed heads of York, Salisbury and several other Yorkist commanders, namely Limbrike, Stanley, Bourchier, Thomas Harrington, William Parr, Pickering, Harrow and Hanson, were according to William of Worcester:

'...affixed in various parts of York, whilst a paper crown was placed in derision on the head of the Duke of York.'[36]

Or as Polydore Vergil wrote:

'...were carried to Yorke for a spectacle to the people, and a terror to the rest of their adversaryes.'[37]

Once these severed heads were mounted along various parts of the city of York, Margaret ordered, that a sign be placed below the severed head of the Duke of York – which had been placed above Micklegate Bar – on which, it is claimed the following words had been written:

'Let York Overlook York.'

It is also said that she ordered that there be sufficient space left between the heads of Salisbury and Hanson in anticipation of also placing the heads of the Earl of Warwick and the Earl of March, sometime in the future.

Finally a paper crown was affixed to the head of the Duke of York, in mocking reference to his claim to the throne. With this concluding act, the Wakefield campaign came to an end and the ground was laid for the Towton campaign.

The coat of arms of the victorious Queen Margaret.

The reader should be aware that there are alternative versions to the battle of Wakefield and these are examined in detail in the author's book, **The Battle of Wakefield 1460** by Philip Haigh, published by Sutton Publishing Ltd, £18.99. ISBN 0-7509-1342-8.

The version presented here in **From Wakefield to Towton** is considered by Philip Haigh and the Battleground Britain designers to be the account which most closely fits the available evidence.

Chapter Four

The 1461 Campaign

The march south

FOLLOWING THE LANCASTRIAN VICTORY at Wakefield, there was a joining up at York with Margaret of Anjou and her army of Scottish/Northern mercenaries. It was then time for the Lancastrian commanders to liberate King Henry VI from his Yorkist protectors in London. Early in January, they set off with their whole army – heading south – along the 'Great North Road'. Although the Lancastrians could boast to have much of the nobility of the land amongst their ranks, and they marched under the banner of the Prince of Wales with his emblems of the white swan and ostrich feather, their army, particularly the northern mercenaries, was nothing more than a rabble.

It appears that the Lancastrian commanders – who were short of funds – allowed the mercenaries amongst their rank, a free hand as they passed through any town south of the Trent river. This 'march' south, is well chronicled, an account of the widespread plundering by the Lancastrians as they marched to St. Albans can be found in C. L.Scofield's, *The Life and Reign of Edward IV*, 1923, Vol. I, (pages 135 – 136). See also *Gregory's Chronicle*, (page 212) and *English Chronicle*, (page 107).

This 'permission to pillage' was to severely damage what little favourable public opinion the Lancastrians held with the population south of the River Trent, and was to bring massive destruction to most of the towns along the 'Great North Road', particularly those which were known to be supportive to the Yorkist cause, Grantham, Stamford, Peterborough, Huntingdon, Melbourn and Royston suffered particularly due to their strong Yorkist loyalties and connections, as the Lancastrian army slowly marched nearer to London.

The following chronicle of the prior of Croyland Abbey describes the destruction that the Lancastrians wrought:

> 'The duke [of York] being thus removed from this world, the northemen, being sensible that only impediment was now withdrawn, and that there was no one now who would care to resist their inroads, again swept onwards like a whirlwind from the north, and in the impulse of their fury attempted to overrun the whole of England...
>
> 'Thus did they proceed with impunity, spreading in vast multitudes over a space of thirty miles in breadth [either side of the 'Great North Road'] and, covering the whole surface of the earth just like a plague of Locusts, made their way almost to the very walls of London; all the movables which they could possibly collect in every quarter placed on

beasts of burden and carried off.

'With such avidity for spoil they did press on, that they dug up precious vessels which, through fear of them, had been concealed in the earth, and with threats of death compelled the people to produce the treasures which they had hidden in remote and obscure spots.

'What do you suppose must have been our fears dwelling here in this island, when every day rumours of this sad nature were reaching our ears, and we were in the utmost dread that we should have to experience similar hardships to those which had been inflicted by them upon our neighbours...'[1]

The Second Battle of St. Albans

Meanwhile, the Earl of Warwick, apparently informed of the disaster which had befallen the Yorkists at Wakefield, and despite the sorrow of losing not only his father, brother, uncle and cousin, began mustering his forces ready to repel the 'northern hoards'. His scouts and informers were telling him that the Lancastrians were approaching the capital.

In the second week in February, 1461, the number of Yorkists gathered in London increased appreciably as news spread of the destruction brought about by Margaret's northern army. They now sought protection from the one man whom they felt could make a stand against them – the Earl of Warwick. With a small army gathered to him he left the city and began to march north, to face the Lancastrians in battle.

The Lancastrians defeated the Yorkists at the Second Battle of St Albans and captured King Henry VI. The close-quarter nature of mediaeval fighting and the weaponry used meant appalling injuries for the participants.

At the same time, many of the citizens who had remained in London began to bury their possessions and secure their premises and an air of fear settled over the city as each man woman and child contemplated the outcome of the forthcoming conflict. Meanwhile, the Earl of Warwick, unsure of exactly where the Lancastrians would appear, set up a defensive perimeter around St. Albans and waited for the arrival of Margaret's army. The Lancastrians fell upon the Yorkists at St. Albans on the 17 February, and in the engagement that followed, the Lancastrians 'rolled up' the Yorkists left flank, stationed around St. Albans itself, and totally routed the remaining Yorkists. In this encounter, the Earl of Warwick, and many of the other Yorkist commanders, managed to escape.

However, the Earl of Warwick had rashly decided to take Henry VI with him on the St. Albans campaign, and in the confusion of the rout of the Yorkist army, Henry was left behind and so found himself reunited with his wife Margaret and his young son Edward. The situation was looking rosey for the House of Lancaster.

The Earl of Warwick and the portion of his army that he had managed to keep intact after the rout at St. Albans, retreated into the Cotswolds. There he was reunited with the new Duke of York, Edward, Earl of March, and duke's own forces. Edward had learned of his father's defeat and death at Wakefield. He was flush with victory having commanded an army which had just defeated a Welsh Lancastrian force at Mortimer's Cross on 2 February. Now he was marching east to come to the aid of the Earl of Warwick. When Edward and Warwick met, it is said that Edward, after realising that Warwick had 'lost' Henry VI in the rout at St. Albans, reportedly shouted at Warwick '...where is the king?...'. To which the calm and collected Warwick replied, '...but my Lord, you are the king!'. If this is true, then even at this point, the politically astute Earl of Warwick was already planning how best to turn the defeat and death of the Duke of York and the 'loss' of Henry VI to his advantage.

The Lancastrian return to the North

Realising that the road to London was open to the Lancastrians, the two Yorkist commanders decided to march their combined forces towards the capital. However, the Lancastrians were unable to take full advantage of the Yorkist defeat, and gain the inniative after the battle of St. Albans. They did advance on London, but their reputation had gone before them, and the Londoners, fearful of what the Lancastrian soldiers would do if they had a free hand in the city, closed the city gates. Thus their King and the Lancastrian commanders and nobles were barred along with the from entry into the city. Rather than attempting to take London by storm, the Lancastrians – who were camped at Barnet – decided that they should return to the Lancastrian heartlands in the north. There they would regroup and plan their next course of action. They turned their army around and began the long march north towards the city of York.

It was the refusal to allow the Lancastrians access to the capital, and their subsequent decision to withdraw north, which was to prove to be the turning point in the struggles between the two warring houses. The last twelve months for the Yorkists had been a roller-coaster ride for them in terms of fortunes: they had swung from their lowest point, the flight from Ludford Bridge, to their highest, their return from exile and control of the crown by capturing Henry VI at Northampton. Then, back to another low with the Duke of York's death at Wakefield, where they not only lost their figurehead, but after being found on the losing side of two major military engagements, also lost control of the person of King Henry VI, as well as the death of a

The citizens of London closed the gates to the Lancastrian hordes fearful of what the soldiers would do. News of their appalling behaviour on the march from the north of England had gone before them. Map dated 1572. King Henry VI was thus banned from his own capital, along with his Lancastrian supporters, and the ground was laid for the acceptance of another monarch.

number of their key military advisors.

However, their fortunes were once again to change for the better when the Yorkists' commanders Edward and Warwick and their supporters, entered the capital 26 February 1461. Clearly, along the way from the Cotswolds, Warwick had convinced Edward that this was the right time to declare himself king. The Duke of York was dead, and under the 'Act of Accord' his heir (Edward) could claim the throne after Henry VI had died. The fact that Henry was alive and well, did not stop them from declaring it anyway, and they claimed that Henry and his supporters had already breached the agreement laid down in the act by causing:

> 'long before...[Edward's arrival in London]... unrest, inward war and trouble, unrightwiseness, shedding and effusion of innocent blood, abusion of the laws, partiality, riot, ectortion, murder, rape and vicious living have been the guiders and leader of the noble realm of England...'[2]

It was at this point that they called upon the citizens of London to accept Edward not only as their king, but to be their saviour from the rampaging Lancastrians, no doubt lingering on the fact that they could put a stop to the aforementioned rape and murder. This appears to have worked, for the citizens perceived Edward, who was young, dynamic and certainly more popular than the late Richard Duke of York, a more suitable candidate for king than Henry or Richard and readily agreed. Therefore, from that day on, Edward was know as Edward IV, King of England. The following chronicle describes his accession to the throne:

> 'And upon the Thursday following th'Earls of March and of Warwick with a great power of men, entered the city of London, the which of the citizens joyously received, and upon the Sunday following the said earl caused to be mustered his people in St. John's Field, where unto that host were proclaimed and shewed certain articles and points that King Henry had offended in, whereupon it was demanded of the said people whether the said Henry were worthy to reign as king any longer or no. Whereupon the people cried hugely and said, Nay, Nay.
>
> 'And after it was asked of them whether they would have th'Earl of March for their king and they cried with one voice, Yea, Yea. After the which admission thus by the commons assented, certain captains were assigned to bear report thereof unto the said Earl of March, then being lodged at his place called Baynard's Castle. Of the which when he was by them ascertained he thanked God and them...' [3]

Despite this popular acclaim, there was still the issue of the Lancastrian army in the north to deal with – coupled with the fact that there were now two kings of England. The morale of the Lancastrian army was exceptionally high at this point. With two victories behind them, the death of the Duke of York and the release of the King Henry VI, who could blame them. Clearly, the Lancastrian strategy had changed, as Goodman mentions in his work, *The Wars of the Roses*, where he writes:

> 'The Wakefield campaign reveals a new style of military leadership among the Yorkists' opponents – devious, inventive and quick to exploit opportunities. The complacency shown by York and Salisbury over Christmas may have stemmed partly from a failure to grasp that they were dealing with opponents no longer prepared to keep faith with them...
>
> 'The Lancastrians had, indeed, recently lost some of their most experienced and forceful captains (Buckingham, Shrewsbury, Beaumont and Egremont); and two of their present commanders, Somerset and Exeter, had recently failed dismally. The quality of the northern command was again demonstrated after Wakefield in their ability and determination to launch an invasion of the south in mid-winter, culminating in a second victory only seven weeks after the first...' [4]

The Yorkists were equally aware of this, and with this as a back drop to their activities they began assembling their forces and planning their march north to confront the Lancastrians, and settle the dynastic issue once and for all. However, unlike his father Richard, the newly crowned Edward IV was prepared for the conflict to come. Boardman, wrote in *The Battle of Towton 1461*:

> 'The war between north and south was to continue, but with a new slant in the form of a man who was prepared, with the help of his followers, to usurp the English throne. Unlike his father, Richard Duke of York, Edward was no longer prepared to keep faith with his enemies – his father's killers – or the king. However, he saw the means, with Warwick's political prowess, if not his military ability, to assert his own

Richard's son, Edward crowned King of England by popular acclaim of the citizens of London. There were now two rival kings – the Lancastrian Henry VI and the new Yorkist monarch, Edward IV. Far from being over with the death of Richard, the feuding between the two families was hotting up.

character on the Londoners in the guise of a medieval saviour, now that they were desperate for deliverance. He was about not only to bring his father's claims back to life, but also to surpass them, fighting the bloodiest battle on British soil in the process.' [5]

The Yorkist Call to Arms

No sooner had Edward formally declared himself King of England at Westminster Abbey 4 March 1461, than he at once began to display the determination which was synonymous with the early years of his reign. He immediately began issuing proclamations, first he called upon the sheriffs of thirty-three English counties (all except one were south of the River Trent and in the Yorkist heartlands) to accept him as king and offer no support to the Lancastrians. He also stated that if any Lancastrian submitted within ten days then they would be pardoned. This was with the exception of a predetermined list of men mentioned by name and anybody with an income of more than 100 marks a year. This was a clever attempt by Edward to win over the common man at the expense of the richer Lancastrian nobility. Commissions of Arrays were issued and the fledgling king set about gathering as large an army that was possible in the winter months to confront the Lancastrians.

To assist in this, a number of the Yorkist nobles left the capital to gather men on Edward's behalf. On 7 March Warwick left London to recruit from his estates in the midlands. Likewise, other notable Yorkist commanders such as Robert Horne and John Fogge travelled to Kent to do the same – as did the Duke of Norfolk, who, although in ill health, assured Edward that although he would have to catch the king up (on his march north) he would come with a large force recruited from his estates in and around Norfolk and East Anglia.

The Yorkists march North

The Yorkist army began leaving London 11 March 1461. The first to leave was Lord Fauconberg at the head of Edward's vanguard, a force made up of Welshmen, men that had been with him at Mortimer's Cross. Edward himself left two days later on the 13th with the main part of the army following the established route north along the Great North Road. This also included a force of hand gunners sent across the English Channel by the Duke of Burgundy who was keen to establish and maintain a good relationship with the new king. They followed the same route that the Duke of York had taken the previous year. The army progressed at a deliberately moderate pace (to allow others to join or catch up with the main force) and on 16 March, Edward reached St. Albans – the scene of the Yorkists most recent defeat. By the 17th, they had reached Cambridge and on 22 March, (according to John de Waurin's account of the campaign) they arrived at Nottingham.

Throughout that trek, the ranks of Edward's army were swelled by many

Edward's banner

men all rallying to the Yorkist king's call to arms. The success of the original muster in London, and it's continuing success on Edward's march north was captured in a contemporary poem titled 'The Rose of Rouen' (the 'rose' being Edward and 'Rouen' being an obvious reference to his birthplace), written shortly after the events of 1461. In it, it demonstrates just how much support Edward had – and a portion goes as follows:

'For to save all England The Rose did his intent,
With Calais and with London with Essex and with Kent,
And all the south of England up to the water of Trent,
And when he saw the time best The Rose from London went,
Blessed be the time, that ever God spread the flower!

The way into the north country The Rose full fast he sought,
With him went the Ragged Staff [Earl of Warwick] that many men
there brought,
So did the White Lion [Duke of Norfolk] full worthy he wrought,
Almighty Jesus bless his soul, that their armies taught,
Blessed be the time, that ever God spread that flower!

The Fish Hook [Lord Fauconberg] came to the field in full eager
mood,
So did the Cornish Chough [Lord Scrope of Bolton] and brought
forth all her brood,
There was the Black Ragged Staff [Lord Grey of Ruthin] that is
both true and good,
The Bridled Horse [Sir William Herbert], the Water Boughet
[Viscount Bouchier] by the Horse stood [Earl of Arundel].
Blessed be the time, that ever God spread that flower!

The Greyhound [Sir Walter Devereux], the Harts Head [Lord
Stanley] they quit them well that day,
So did the Harrow of Canterbury and Clinton [Lord Clinton] with
his Key,
The white ship of Bristol he feared not the fray,

The Black Ram of Coventry he said not one nay,
Blessed be the time, that ever God spread that flower!

The Falcon and the Fetterlock [Edward as Duke of York] was
there that tide,
The Black Bull [Sir William Hastings] also himself would not hide,
The Dolphin [Lord Audley] came from Wales, three Corbies [Sir
Roger Corbie] by his side,
The proud Leopard of Salisbury gaped his eyes wide,
Blessed be the time, that ever God spread that flower!

The Wolf came from Worcester, full sore he thought to bite,
The Dragon came from Gloucester, he bent his tail to smite,
The Griffen came from Leicester, flying in as tight,
The George came from Nottingham, with spear for to fight,
Blessed be the time, that ever God spread that flower!' [6]

It was when Edward's main force had crossed the Trent (some time after 18 March) that his force was joined by those recruited by the Earl of Warwick. Warwick was in jubilant mood. While he had been at Coventry recruiting for the Yorkist cause, his men had captured and subsequently executed the 'Bastard of Exeter' – William Holland – illegitimate son of Sir Henry Holland, Duke of Exeter, whom, it had been said, had been one of those responsible for Warwick's father's (the Earl of Salisbury) execution the previous December at Pontefract Castle.

The subject of Pontefract Castle must have featured several times in the conversations of the Yorkist command as they travelled north. As the Duke of York had planned to use that location as a base of operations in the 1460 campaign, before being side tracked to Sandal, then equally, it was well placed to serve as a Yorkist one in the 1461 campaign. That the Lancastrians were in the north was not disputed by the Yorkist command, indeed, their approximate location in Yorkshire was probably well known to them (although this cannot be proved), as undoubtedly, the Yorkists would have had many spies and scouts ahead of them reporting back on a regular basis. Pontefract Castle would make an ideal location from whence to launch the war in Yorkshire against the Lancastrians and it is not unreasonable to suggest that the decision to go there was thus consciously made. It has been suggested by other historians that in the same way that the Duke of York had ordered the Royal Artillery to be taken from London on his campaign, in case Pontefract Castle was held against them, that indeed Edward ordered the same. However, unlike his father's campaign, whereby the artillery had to be returned to London because poor weather had made the roads impassable, in this instance they remained with either the rearguard or the baggage train. Their immediate worry however, was the structure of the army.

Although the poem 'The Rose of Rouen' reads as an impressive list of nobles present in Edward's army, and towns and cities who offered support in terms of both men, arms and money, it should be noted that with the exception of the Duke of Norfolk, the Earls of Arundel, Warwick, and Lord Fauconberg, there was very little high ranking nobility in Edward's army. In fact it is fair to say that Edward relied heavily on the support of the common man and lesser nobles to assist him in the coming campaign. This is in stark contrast to the support that the Lancastrians could muster.

It should be noted that the poem in no way presents a comprehensive list of Yorkist surporters. John Neville, Lord Montagu (Warwick's brother), Sir John Wenlock, Sir John Dinham, Sir Walter Blount, John de la Pole, Sir Humphrey Stafford, Lord Grey of Wilton, Lord Dudley, Sir Robert Ogle, Sir William Stanley to name only a few, were also present in Edward's army and are not mentioned in the poem.

Edward himself led the middle, they had had little or no word from the Duke of Norfolk, who was supposed to make up the rearguard with his contingent from Norfolk. Although Edward's army numbered into the many thousands, the Lancastrian numbered many more. Any battle fought without the Duke of Norfolk would start with the Yorkists being more than a little disadvantaged – a sobering thought for the Yorkists as they continued their march north to face the Lancastrians.

Edward, the once Earl of March, now the new Duke of York after his father's death at Wakefield, at eighteen years of age was an accomplished commander. He set about seeking vengeance for his father and his beloved younger brother, Edmund, Earl of Rutland, who had been murdered on Wakefield bridge by 'Butcher' Clifford.

Lancastrian activity in Yorkshire

But in the meantime, what were the Lancastrians doing? We should not doubt that the Lancastrian command was aware of the Yorkists' activity in the south. They would have soon heard that Edward was recruiting and were probably aware of the date of his departure from London. They had a number of experienced soldiers with them, and many knew the area in and around Yorkshire well. Therefore, they held the advantage of being able to wait for the Yorkists to come to them and had plenty of time to choose the ground upon which they would face them. They would have been equally well aware that the area of ground between the villages of Saxton and Towton fifteen miles south-west of the city of York, by which the little River Cock flowed – upon which they could anchor their right flank – was a tactically excellent location. It was close to York, Pontefract and many other sizable settlements and straddled a major road network. The actual date when the Lancastrians arrived and camped their army at Towton is unknown, but it would certainly have taken several days to gather the whole army at that place. But once gathered, from here they could organise the collecting of food and provisions to feed their army, and at the same time, prepare the ground for the battle to come.

There is an unanswered question here to be considered. Would the Lancastrians have kept a standing army in the field for over a cold winter's month? Clearly, a large number of nobles would have stayed within the relative comfort of the city of York, but what about the foot soldiers? The probability is that many were dispersed, and as the Yorkist force approached they were called back again to muster under Henry VI's banner, if not at Towton then perhaps at York. Either way, in the last week in March, the army did come together and formed up on the chosen ground between Towton and Saxton.

It should also be noted, that not only did the Lancastrians plan to use the River Cock to shield their right flank, but in order to hamper any planned Yorkist flanking attacks, all the bridges over the river to the rear of their lines were planned to be broken down to make them unusable by the Yorkists once the Lancastrians had crossed over them enroute to the Towton area. Not only this, but in order to make it as difficult as possible for the Yorkists to meet them at Towton, they also planned one further surprise, they would make the Yorkists pay dearly for any crossing over the River Aire to the south of the Lancastrian position. All they had to do was wait and see where the Yorkists would attempt to cross the river.

The Great Seals of the two contenders for the throne of England, left Henry VI and right Edward IV

Chapter Five

The Battle of Ferrybridge

The Yorkists arrive at Pontefract

THE STRATEGICALLY POSITIONED and formidable Pontefract Castle was to be the Yorkist base of operations in the north in their campaign against the Lancastrians. Edward duly arrived there some time on the 27 March, and, his army camped on the triangular piece of land below the castle known locally as 'Bubwith Heath' – now on the Knottingley Road.

At the time of the Battle of Wakefield three months previously, clearly the castle at Pontefract had been in Lancastrian hands. There is however, no mention of any resistance to the Yorkist arrival at Pontefract Castle or of a hostile Lancastrian garrison. Therefore it has to be concluded that either the keeper of the castle was sympathetic to the Yorkist cause, or that by this time the castle had been abandoned.

Further, it is not known when it was that the Yorkists learned that the Lancastrian army was actually located between the villages of Towton and Saxton, but as both sides had their scouts and spies, they would have surely been aware of each other's whereabouts. That being the case, the Yorkists' next objective, having established a base of operations at Pontefract, was to secure a protected crossing point over the River Aire. With that objective in mind, the Yorkists despatched a small force to seize and hold the river crossing at Ferrybridge, an action that set in motion the Battle of Ferrybridge.

The first attack on Ferrybridge – Afternoon 27th March, 1461

Edward ordered John Radcliffe, Lord Fitzwalter and Warwick's illegitimate brother, 'The Bastard of Salisbury', to advance to the crossing with a small force (number unknown) and to seize the bridge over the River Aire at this point, a bridge which may or may not have been intact at this time. The matter of whether the bridge was 'broken' or not, is a subject of debate amongst historians. On the one hand it could be argued that Edward sent Fitzwalter to repair the bridge, as the Lancastrians had broken it down. On the other hand, it could be argued that Edward sent Fitzwalter to capture an intact bridge and hold it until the main army arrived.

It is likely however, that the bridge was guarded by a Lancastrian contingent. It would make military sense to do so and as shall be seen, the bridge was held in sufficiently high regard by the Lancastrians to mount an attack on it the following morning as part of their plan to make the Yorkist pay for crossing the river.

The original Yorkist force under Fitzwalter's command duly arrived at the bridge and what followed, can only be described in military terms as a skirmish whereby the Yorkists forcibly drove off the defending Lancastrians.

It was relatively late on in the day of the 27th, as Fitzwalter had to camp there for the night. We can conclude that it was too late in the day for him to return to the comfort of Pontefract Castle. So he choose to camp there, at Ferrybridge, with his command, and protect the prize that he had captured for his king.

The second attack on Ferrybridge – Morning 28th March

Lancastrian survivors of the encounter would have made it back to the Lancastrian camp at Towton and reported the events to their commanders. Now knowing that Ferrybridge was the chosen crossing point for the Yorkist army, the Lancastrians decided that it was a good place to inflict an opening wound on the Yorkist force. As Edward Hall wrote, the Lancastrians then decided to go on the offensive:

> 'Let no man think or yet imagine, that either the council of King Henry, or his vigilant Queen, either neglected nor forgot to know or search what their enemies did, but they prepared to their power all the men they either could persuade or allure to their purpose to take their part. And thus thinking themselves furnished, committed the governance of the army to the Duke of Somerset, the Earl of Northumberland and the Lord Clifford...
>
> 'These noble captains, leaving King Henry, his wife and son for their safeguard in the city of York, passed the River Wharfe [a reference to the army moving to Towton] with all their power, intending to prohibit King Edward to pass over the River Aire...[and]...the Lord Clifford determined with his light horsemen, to make an assault to such as kept the passage of Ferrybridge, and so departed from the great army on the Saturday before Palm Sunday [the 28th], and early before his enemies were awake, got the bridge, and slew the keepers of the sames and all as would withstand him...' [1]

History has not much more to add to this account, as it would appear that John, Lord Clifford along with John, Lord Neville, did indeed, with a force of some 500 men – probably their own household troops and soldiers – in Clifford's case, 'The Flower of Craven', as tradition has us believe they were called – advanced to Ferrybridge. Very early in the morning on the the 28th, they carried out, what can only be described as a surprise attack on the Yorkist forces ensconced on both sides of the bridge – with apparently some success. Again, Edward Hall goes on to record that:

> 'The Lord Fitzwalter hearing the noise suddenly rose from his bed and unarmed, with a poleaxe in his hand, thinking that it was an affray amongst his men, came down to appease the same, but before he

Some of the types of maces and battle hammers in use during the period of the Wars of the Roses.

> could say a word, or knew what the matter was, he was slain, and with him the Bastard of Salisbury, brother to the Earl of Warwick, a valiant young gentleman, and of great audacity.' [2]

The Lancastrians were back in control of the bridge and prepared to defend it in force. In preparation for this, it is likely that the bridge was broken at this point to aid the Lancastrian defence. The chronicled accounts of the events that followed indicate that after this time the bridge was indeed 'broken'.

Thus, with the bridge destroyed and the north bank of the river held by Clifford and Neville and their respective forces, the Lancastrians were ready to make their stand and face the might of the Yorkist forces that opposed them. In the same way that the Lancastrian survivors of the Yorkist attack on the 27th retreated back to their main force, then so it is true that the Yorkist survivors of this Lancastrian attack did the same.

It is important to understand that by this time the Yorkist army was rising from their billets in and around Pontefract Castle, when the quiet of the winter's morning was shattered by these survivors, when they – no-doubt in 'routing' manner – came fleeing into the Yorkist camp. Bearing in mind that large numbers of the Yorkist rank and file were not professional soldiers, or men-at-arms, we can only imagine the panic that this caused amongst these untrained men, as the stories the survivors told were no doubt exaggerated and it is not to be doubted also, that subsequently a degree of panic rapidly spread through the Yorkist ranks as they feared that the Lancastrians were at that very moment, in large numbers, advancing upon their position.

As it transpired, although the Yorkists did not know it at the time, the reality of the situation was that the Lancastrians, far from taking the fight to the Yorkist camp, were in fact, preparing to defend the river crossing in some strength.

History is riddled with significant moments, and the Towton campaign has a number of it's own. It appears that Warwick, sensing the growing nervousness amongst the Yorkists and fearing the discord would soon turn to panic, followed by a wholesale rout, decided to take matters into his own hands. The events that followed were recorded by Edward Hall:

> 'When the Earl of Warwick was informed of this feat [Clifford and Neville's attack], he like a man desperate, mounted on his hackney, and came blowing to King Edward saying, "Sir I pray God have mercy on their souls, which in the beginning of your enterprise hath lost their lives, and because I see no success of the world, I remit the vengeance and punishment to God our creator and redeemer", and with that he alighted down and slew his horse with his sword, saying, "Let him fly that will, for surely I will tarry with him that will tarry with me" and he kissed the cross hilt of his sword.' [3]

Over the years, much has been made and subsequently debated regarding the Earl of Warwick's military skills. However, there is no doubt about his ability to seize a critical political moment and make the most of it, or in this case, seize the moment and not let it become any worse. On hearing of this dramatic act, which in effect meant that Warwick, by the slaying of his own horse, would stand his ground and take the same risks as the rank and file, there appears to have been a steadying of the nerves on the part of the Yorkist soldiers. A potential rout situation was averted.

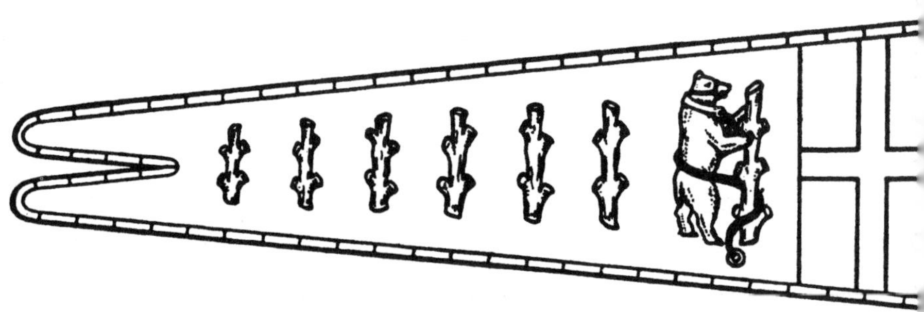

Earl of Warwick's standard.

YORK
Knaresburgh
Hay park
Wetherby
ANSTY
BARKSTON
Bramham
Moore
Sherborn
Woode
WAPONTAK
Ledes
Pontefract
Kridling park
OSGO
AGGBRIGGE
Wakefeilde
WAPONT.
DINGE
STAINCROSE
Barnesley
Tadcaster
Tockwith
Bilton
Nether Poppleto
Over Poppleton
Overton
Newton
Redhouses
Nunmunkton
Akeham
Dringhouses
Middlethorp
Busshopthorp
Coppethorp
Bilburgh
Caterton
Steton hall
Oxton
Belton
Apleton
Nun Appleton
Kirkby
N. Milford
Fenton
Wystow
Towton
Saxton
Barkston
Aberforth
Huddleston
Mickelfeld
Garforth
Barwick in Elmet
Kidhall
Haselwood
Hedley
Thorner
Moreton
Shadwell
Alwoodley
Chappelton
Widkirk
New bigin
Hunslete
Beiston
Middleton
Rodwell
Olton
Ledston
Farbourn
Byrom
Burton
Brotherton
Knottingley
Beall
Kellington
Hensall
Eggbrough
Whitley
Darrington
Womersley
Stapleton
Wentbrig
Norton
Campsall
Smeton
Upton
Burghwalles
Baddesworth
Hemsworth
Elmesall south
Kirkby South
Felkirk
Royston
Darton
Auston
Adwick
Brodesworth
Bilsham
Hickleton
Scausbye
Caswortb
Barnburgh
Derfeild
Newhall
Drax
Dodworth
Cauthorne
Barmby hall
Huland
Wolley
Bretton hall
Netherton
Sandall Ca.
Crofton
Foulby
Wragbye
Nostall
Sharston
Heathe
Warmfield
Normanton
Snydall
Preston
Hardwick
Ackworth
Aketon
Newland
Fetherston
Altofts
Castleford
Houghton
Waterfriston
Methley
Carleton
Stanley
Thorpe
Dunningley
Morley
Adwalton
Farneley
Armley
Horsforth
Kersal
Rigton
Harwood
Gauthrop Hall
Castel
Watersham
Collingham
Clyfford
Newton
Smauis
Oggle thorp
Bramham
Walton
Bikerton
Spoforth
Spoforth park
S. Dighton
N. Dighton
Sickling
Lynton
Kirkby
Weton
Almoscliff
Rigton
Pannell
Plompto towre
Follyfote
Gouldesburgh
Whixley
Allerton Maleuery
Kirk Hamerton
Cathall
Hunsingnor
Walkingham
Copgrave
Burton leonard
Ingrethorp
Stanley
Marton
Arkedal
Ouse flu
Usbornes
Nether Dunsford
Over Dunsford
Skotton
Skreuen
Brearton
Hatgate
Doncaster

The third attack on Ferrybridge – Afternoon 28 March 1461

Shortly after these events, a Yorkist council of war was held and the decision was made to retake the crossing. Indeed if they wished to face the Lancastrians in a full scale battle on this occasion, it was a military necessity. It was agreed that Warwick, no doubt as a result of his earlier speech, would be best suited to lead the attack and the Yorkists prepared to advanced towards the bridge in force, for what would become the third and final assault on Ferrybridge. Further, Edward Hall in *Hall's Chronicle*, suggests that at this point, in the same way that Henry V raised the spirits of his troops with a stirring speech before the battle of Agincourt, Edward IV himself spoke to his troops offering them a chance to depart with honour or to stay and share in the fabulous riches that the victory against the Lancastrians would bring, adding that an extra reward would be paid for those who captured deserters from the Yorkist forces.

It took some time to get the Yorkist army on the move, and it is likely that it was not much before noon that the Yorkists were in a position to attack the Lancastrians at Ferrybridge. When they finally got there, they found the bridge broken and the Lancastrians holding the north banks in force. The engineers were called and no doubt at this point, due to the fact that the two sides could not get involved in actual hand to hand combat, an archery duel commenced. It was concluded that by using the remains of the bridge and such suitable items that could be found in the immediate vicinity, a narrow crossing could be made across the river. Whilst the archery duel raged around them, Yorkist soldiers and engineers slowly manoeuvred forward under the cover of shields and protective barriers to bridge the broken section. This would allow advance elements of their army to charge across to the other side and engage in hand to hand combat with the Lancastrians.

We are told that in attempting this the Yorkists suffered many casualties, as the hastily built makeshift structure edged it's way ever forward over the gap in the broken bridge. As men tried to get to the other side, in the crush and probably due to the fact that they were traversing an unstable structure under enemy fire, many were caused to fall into the freezing water, killing large numbers as a consequence. The battle carried on for some time, but no matter how determined the Yorkists attacks became, they could not force a crossing. It is said that even a direct assault led by Warwick himself failed to force a way and he too was forced to retreat, beaten back by resolute

Pikeman's helmet dating from the period of the Wars of the Roses.

Lancastrian defence. Warwick sustained an arrow wound to the leg in the process. On this subject of the battle of Ferrybridge and Warwick's injury, Gregory in his chronicle wrote:

> 'And on the 28th March, that was Palm Sunday eve, the Lord Fitzwalter was slain at Ferrybridge and many with him were slain and drowned. And the Earl of Warwick was hurt in his leg with an arrow at the same time...' [4]

Fauconberg's flanking attack

With casualties mounting and time passing, it became clear that an alternative tactic would be required in order to force a crossing of the river. The Yorkist commanders were aware that several miles down river at Castleford there was a ford which could be used to traverse the river. Lord Fauconberg and several other Yorkist nobles were instructed to take a contingent of Yorkist cavalry down to Castleford, cross the river, and attack the Lancastrians in the flank. Hall mentions this in his account and states:

> '...the Lord Fauconberg, Sir Walter Blount and Robert Horne, with the foreward, passed the river at Castleford three miles from Ferrybridge, intending to have environed and enclosed Lord Clifford and his company, but they being therof advertised, departed in great haste towards King Henry's army.' [5]

At what point in the battle this decision was taken is unknown. It could have been at the start of the battle, and the river assault carried out just to keep the Lancastrians occupied. It could have been later, when it became clear that a river assault alone would not force the crossing. Either way, Fauconberg with his cavalry, a force put at less than a thousand men, duly made it to Castleford, crossed the river and began circumnavigating Brotherton Marsh (which is located north of the Aire to the East of Castleford) in preparation to swoop down on the Lancastrian ranks.

Clifford and the Lancastrian John, Lord Neville were not without their own scouts, and they were alerted to the fact that the Yorkists had got behind them. Faced with both a frontal assault and Falconberg's cavalry threatening their line of retreat, they decided that this was the point at which they should retire back to the safety of the main Lancastrian army. The order was given to withdraw back to the Towton area.

The deaths of Neville, Clifford and the 'Flower of Craven'

The exact sequence of events that followed after this, (and for that matter the exact location) are difficult to establish with any degree of certainty. It appears that Clifford and Neville and their force, while trying desperately to reach the safety of the main Lancastrian force, were caught during their retreat by Fauconberg's cavalry. This took place somewhere between Ferrybridge and Saxton, but most probably near to Dintingdale. This a shallow valley that crosses the Ferrybridge-Tadcaster road to Towton, below the plateau where the massive Lancastrian army is said to have camped

John Lord Clifford GW

before the battle and is located south of Towton and about 2 $\frac{1}{2}$ miles south from the village itself, and – according to Edward Hall – in the mêlèe that followed:

'...Lord Clifford, either from heat or pain, put off his gorget [armoured neck protection], was suddenly hit by an arrow, as some say, without a head...

This would have been a bodkin arrow. In effect this was a headless arrow with a cross cut in to the flat edge, in such a manner that when it hit the body the cross would open up and spread out inside the body in the same way that a 'dum dum' bullet does today. A direct hit in the neck from one of these as here suggested by Edward Hall would certainly have caused Clifford to die instantaneously.

'...and was stricken in the throat, and incontinent rendered his spirit. And the Earl of Westmoreland's brother [John Neville] and all his company almost were slain, at a place called Dintingdale, not far from Towton.' [6]

It would appear that the death of both John, Lord Neville and John, Lord Clifford near to Dintingdale brought about the end of the battle of Ferrybridge and ushered in the start of the more famously known battle of Towton.

It is due to the close proximity of both battles (Ferrybridge ending on the 28th and Towton starting on the 29th), and the huge consequences of the battle of Towton, that this somewhat explains why Ferrybridge seems to have been, at best, relegated to a footnote of the battle of Towton, and at worst, in many cases ignored. The confusion of the chroniclers and historians both past and present does nothing to assist the modern historian, indeed it has all too well helped to hinder our understanding of the true nature and sequence of events of this short but ferocious engagement as demonstrated by the following contemporary document, written shortly after the battle of Towton, by the Earl of

Garter stall plate of 'turncoat' Richard Neville GW

Warwick's brother (George Neville), who wrote:

'And at length on Palm Sunday, near a town called Ferrybridge, about sixteen miles from York, our enemies were routed and broken in pieces. Our adversaries had broken the bridge which was our way across, and were strongly posted on the other side, so that our men could only cross by a narrow way which they had made themselves after the bridge was broken. But our men forced a way by sword, and many were slain on both sides. Finally the enemy took to flight, and very many of them were slain as they fled.' [7]

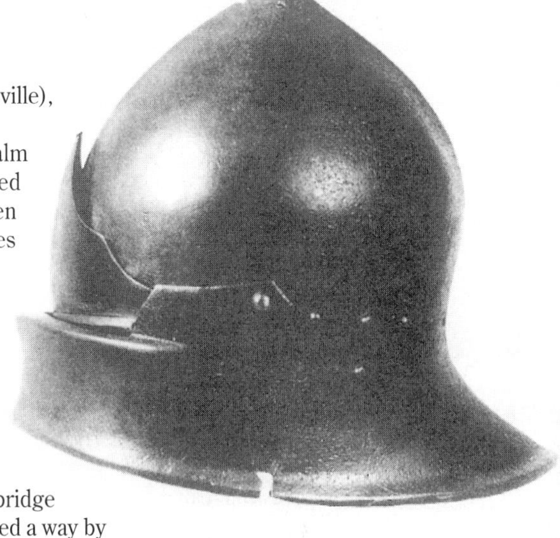

Type of helmet known as the Sallet, usually worn by knights.

From reading this, we could conclude that the battle at Ferrybridge took place on Palm Sunday, which is clearly not the case (as this is the date on which the battle of Towton itself took place), and that there was just one single engagement – which is also not the case. It should not be doubted that Ferrybridge was indeed a battle in its own right. If we are to believe Jean de Waurin, then more soldiers died at the battle of Ferrybridge than at the battle of Wakefield. He wrote:

'...and it so happened the battle lasted from midday to six o'clock in the evening and there died more than 3,000 men on both sides.' [8]

The Yorkist march to Saxton

We know it was late in the day when the Yorkist army finally managed to cross the river. We must remember that it was the end of the winter and the days were still relativly short with night falling at about 7-30pm. With that in mind, we can only imagine the scene that presented itself to anyone who witnessed it: lines of soldiers many weary from the battle at Ferrybridge and many more from the fatigue caused by the long march from London, moving slowly up the road from Ferrybridge towards Towton. Scouts had reported, hundreds maybe thousands of camp fires on and about the ground in and around the village of Towton indicated the vicinity of where the Lancastrians had chosen their ground. Clearly the Saxton/Towton area was the destination for the trudging Yorkists. Jean de Waurin gives us an insight to this, and in his account writes,

'...it was so cold, with snow and ice it was pitiful to see men and horses suffer, especially as they were so badly fed...' [9]

It must have been a worrying time for the Yorkist command, their army strung out in a long line of march. Edward's army no longer marched in the cohesive customary manner of vanguard, mainguard and rearguard. The battle of Ferrybridge – particularly after Fauconberg's advance via Castleford, had caused the army to become disorganised. Much of the vanguard may have followed Fauconberg and was advancing on the Saxton area via Castleford, probably using the old Roman road. As for Fauconberg's cavalry, they may themselves already have arrived in the Saxton area some time earlier – having remained in advance of the main force after their defeat of Clifford's and Neville's force.

As for the rearguard, this portion of the army under the command of the Duke of Norfolk, had not yet even arrived at Ferrybridge – and more worryingly, there was no news of their progress or an estimated time of arrival at the proposed battlefield.

Edward's own line of march from Ferrybridge to the Saxton area is clear. His path would follow, almost identically, what is today the A162 and was then the Great North Road. He would have passed through Sherburn-in-Elmet with most of the Yorkist baggage train in accompaniment, making the journey a slow and tortuous one. In their advance towards the Lancastrians, the Yorkists probably chose to go no further than the village of Saxton itself, being unsure of what now lay ahead, as it was clearly too dark to make an accurate assumption as to the best positions to take for the events that would follow on the morrow. As more of the army arrived, using the roads from both Sherburn-in-Elmet and Castleford, the army would have spilled out across adjacent areas and as the night went on, more and more campfires would have been lit as the Yorkists arrived and made camp at such places as Lead, Barkston Ash, Dintingdale as well as Saxton itself – indeed, many of his soldiers may have spent the night of 28 March in and around Sherburn-in-Elmet – finding that the night was now too short and their fatigue too great to go any further that day.

As they arrived in the vicinity of the chosen place of battle and prepared – if only at this stage 'mentally' – to face the Lancastrians, it was obvious that they were worst for wear when compared to that of the enemy. Edward must have known that the following day a major battle of dynastic consequences would be fought, and equally, he must have also known that he had very little time to somehow bring order to his disorganised and tired army and prepare them for battle.

However, despite any despair that Edward may have felt at this time, no doubt the deaths of both 'Butcher' Clifford (his brother's murderer) and the turncoat John, Lord Neville, (whose defection at Wakefield was probably a defining factor in his own father's death), would have certainly inspired Edward to keep both his own, and his follower's spirits high.

A defining moment in the Wars of the Roses was upon him, in less than twenty four hours the matter would be settled – one way or another.

Chapter Six

The Battle of Towton

The opening positions

EARLY ON THE SUNDAY MORNING of 29 March 1461 thousands of men would have stirred themselves, kicked spluttering camp fires into life, and consumed what vitals they had carried with them. Cold, hunger and the fear of battle would have robbed many of them of a good night's sleep as protagonists on both sides contemplated the melee to come. Quantites of strong ale or un-mixed wine, to de-chill the bones, warm the blood and stir the spirits, would have been issued from the bagage train and eagerly quaffed. The sound of men whetting their steel yet again to achieve that all vital edge to their cutting weapons would be a steadily growing noise. Absent would be the usual loud rumble of throaty voices associated with an assembly of thousands of encamped men. The lively soul would have received short shrift from his comrades for now was no time for levity, but for sombre meditation.What fate did the Almighty have in store for them? Some would contemplate the very real possibility of standing before their Maker ere that day was out. And what a miserable day it was for mortal combat – the sooner it was all over, then so much the better!

Prior to forming up and moving off to the field designated for battle many soldiers, on both sides, would have gathered together in prayer to make their peace with God, priests present in each army moving between the various encampments taking confession. It was Palm Sunday, and very early in the morning, as this activity was going on, the bells of York Minster would have been heard calling the faithful together on this holy day. King Henry VI did not want the battle to be fought on Palm Sunday. Polydore Vergil writes:

> 'When King Henry knew that his enemy were at hand, he did not issue forthwith out of his tent, because Palm Sunday (as they call it) being a solumn feast was at hand, upon which he was rather a minded to have pray then fought, that the next day after he might have better success in the field. But it came to pass by means of the soldiers, who, as their manner is, like not upon lingring, that the very self same day, by day break in the morning, after he had with many words exhorted every man to do particulary his duty, he was forced to cause the alarm to be sounded.' [1]

It appears that the commanders on both sides were not so religiously inclined as their king – preparations for battle on both sides continued apace. We know that Henry VI and his wife Margaret of Anjou were left in York, and no doubt Henry spent the early hours of the morning in prayer. As to Margaret's activities at this time, they go unrecorded.

The Lancastrian army, as at Wakefield the previous December, was once again placed under the command of the 24 year old Duke of Somerset, Henry Beaufort, but again, as at Wakefield, the actual tactical decisions were no doubt left to Sir Andrew Trollope whose control of the Lancastrian forces during the Wakefield campaign had led to a most successful outcome for the Lancastrians. Indeed, the Lancastrians – in gratitude for his military abilities – after the second battle of St. Albans, had Trollope knighted. In the Lancastrian ranks, no doubt the many nobles who were present spent the early hours of the morning being dressed in their fine armour and travelling to the battlefield from where they had billeted the previous night, to join their soldiers on the high ground south of Towton. As for the Yorkists' nobles, they too would have been dressed by their attendants and gathered their forces also in readiness to march and confront the enemy.

It is clear that Edward and the Yorkist commanders, and for that matter the Lancastrian command, were well aware of the close proximity of the opposing forces. John de Waurin tells us in his account of how the reports of the Lancastrian muster to the south of Towton was brought to Edward's attention, he writes:

'When the Earl of March, and his lords were told that King Henry was nearby in the fields they rejoiced, for they wished for nothing more but to fight him. The earl called for his captains and told them to put their men in formation and to take their positions before the enemy came too close. And so it was he organised his battles, and he sent some men to look around the area because they were only four miles from the enemy. They did not go very far before they spotted the reconnaissance party of the enemy, and they very quickly returned to the Earl of March to tell him that they had seen large numbers of men at arms in the fields and the banners of King Henry.

'They told him how the enemy was manoeuvring and their position, and when the earl was warned of this he went to his cavalry, which he positioned on the wing, and said to them, "My children, I pray today that we shall be good and loyal to each other because we are fighting for a good cause!" After they had all echoed this thought a messenger came to the earl that the vaward [vanguard] troops of the King

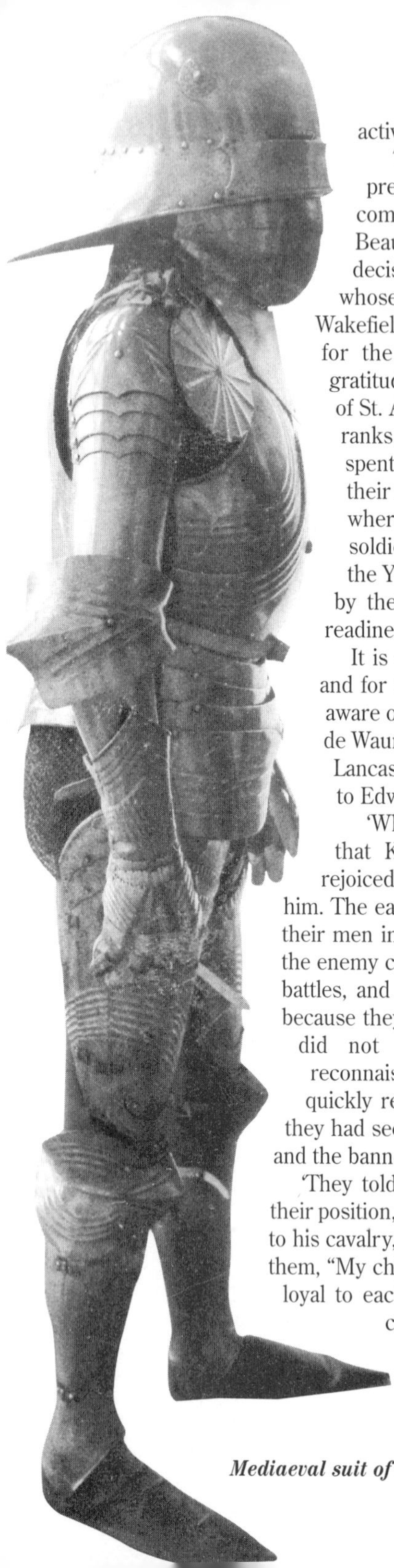

Mediaeval suit of armour. ROYAL ARMOURIES – LEEDS

[Henry] had started to move forward and the earl went back to place himself behind his banners...'[2]

Both sides were hurrying to the chosen place of battle to try and gain the best position for their army. Indeed Polydore Vergil writes, '...his (Henry VI) adversaries were there as ready as he...' leading us to conclude, that even after all their careful planning in the previous weeks, the Lancastrians were nearly caught out at the eleventh hour in regards to getting to their chosen opening position before the Yorkists marched onto the field.

We can only imagine what was going through Edward IV's mind at this time. Although he was in command of a large army, there was still no word from the Duke of Norfolk, and he, along with the other Yorkist commanders, Warwick and Fauconberg, must have realised that as they marched towards the high ground north of Saxton, that the Lancastrians ahead of them outnumbered them. It was still early in the morning when the two forces finally arrived at the chosen field of battle. Edward Hall, in his account of the battle, writes that at 9 o'clock in the morning, the two forces finally came into each other's view and:

> 'When each party perceived each other, they made a great shout, and at the same instant time, there fell a small snyt or snow...'[3]

Several chroniclers mention that it was very cold. The ground would most certainly have been wet – a significant factor later in the battle.

The Lancastrian army occupied the high ground south of Towton village with their right flank anchored on the outskirts of the south of Renshaw Wood – very close to the banks of the River Cock – while their left flank extended across the high ground to the east, and down towards the boggy ground that was present north of Dintingdale, close to a point near to where the current A162 is located. The Yorkist army occupied the high ground north of the village of Saxton, their front extending

Mediaeval suit of armour.
ROYAL ARMOURIES – LEEDS

the full length of the plateau. Both sides were separated by the valley between these two pieces of high ground in which is located – what today is known as – Towton Dale and North Acres. This space of open ground would have kept the opposing forces approximately 400 or so yards apart.

The two sides, rather than deploying on the battlefield in the customary three 'battles' abreast, vanguard to the right, middle in the centre and rearguard to the left, it appears that both armies deployed with the vanguard to the front (which in the case of both armies was made up entirely of archers), the middle behind the vanguard and the rearguard behind that.

For the Yorkists, Lord Fauconberg commanded the vanguard, Warwick commanded the middle and Lords Wenlock and Dinham commanded the rearguard, while Edward himself commanded a reserve – which may or may not have been mounted.

For the Lancastrians the Earl of Northumberland and Sir Andrew Trollope commanded their vanguard, with the Duke of Somerset commanding the middle and some unnamed commander (possibly the Duke of Exeter or some other high ranking noble) commanding the rearguard.

So it came to be that the two forces were finally assembled on the battlefield. As to the numbers present on each side the contemporary and near contemporary chroniclers are at some odds with each other. For the Yorkists, some 20 – 25,000 soldiers on the battlefield (while Norfolk may have had as many as 5,000 somewhere to the rear of the Yorkist position) and the Lancastrian force was probably slightly larger than that of the Yorkists, with somewhere in the region of 30 – 35,000 soldiers present on the field of battle at the start of the conflict.

The opening moves

The snow and prevailing wind was blowing into the faces of the Lancastrians – in a northerly direction. The Yorkist vanguard was made up of archers under command of Lord Fauconberg. He realised that the weather conditions had placed the Yorkists at an advantage. Consequently, he immediately set in motion a string of orders that would take full advantage of this fact. In regards to what happened next, this was recorded by Edward Hall as follows:

> 'The Lord Falconberg, which led the forward...of much experience...caused every archer under his standard to shoot one flight [of arrows] and then made them stand still. The northern men [the Lancastrians] feeling the shot, but by reason of the snow not knowing the distance between them and their enemy, like hardy men, shot their sheaves of arrows as fast as they might, but all their shot was lost [fell short due to the head wind] and their labour was in vain.
>
> 'When their shot was almost spent, the Lord Fauconberg marched forward with his archers, which not only shot their own whole sheaves [of arrows], but also gathered the arrows of their enemies, [a similar tactic was employed by the English at the battle of Poitiers] and let a

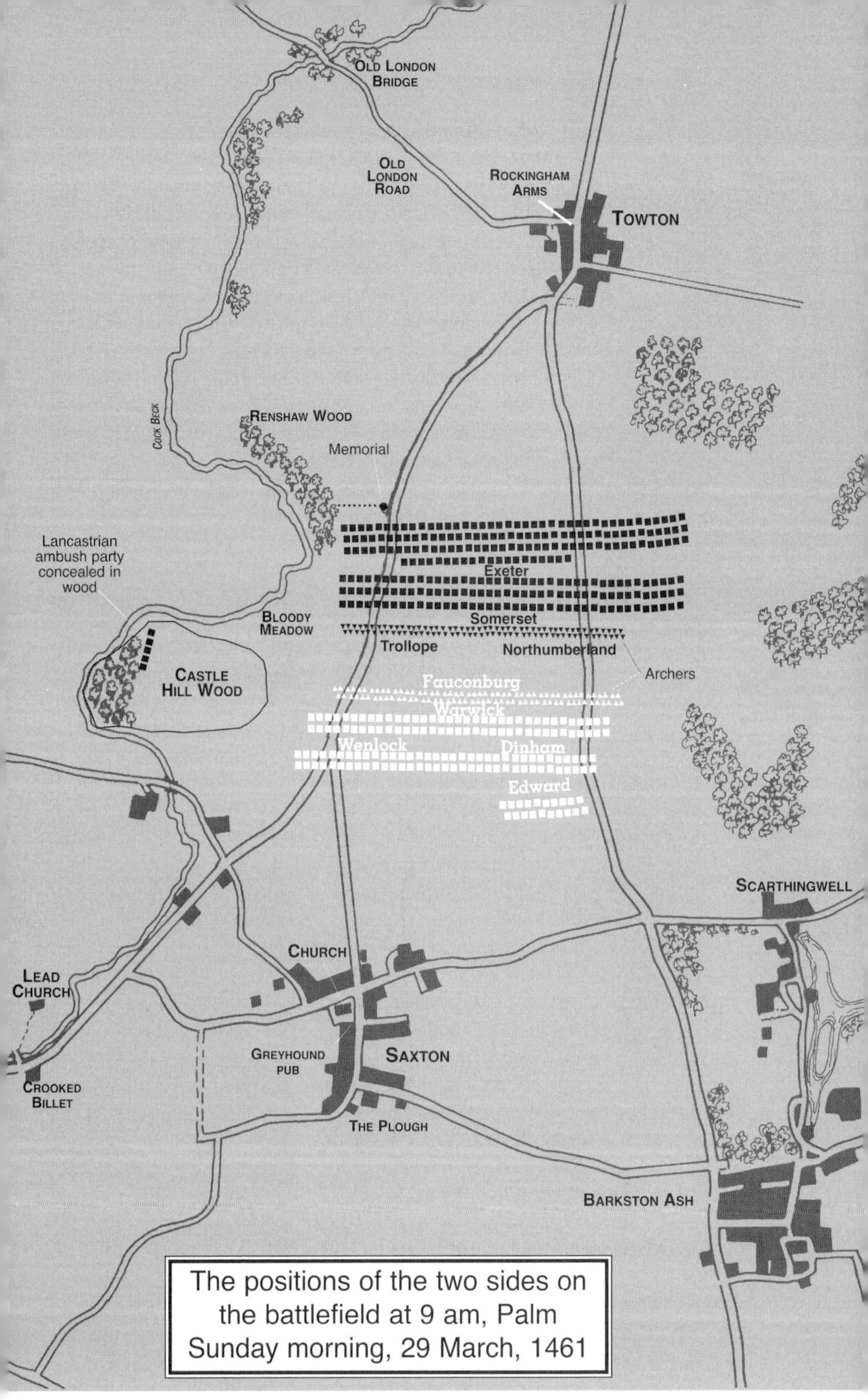

The positions of the two sides on the battlefield at 9 am, Palm Sunday morning, 29 March, 1461

A Yorkist archer. ROYAL ARMOURIES – LEEDS

great part of them fly against their own masters...' [4]

This was a stroke of genius by Fauconberg, whose initial arrow fire had caused the Lancastrians to loose all their own arrows, assuming that because the Yorkists could hit them (and not being able to view the enemy clearly due to the snow blowing in their faces) that they could hit the Yorkists – which was clearly not the case due to the prevailing winds. The return fire by Fauconberg, probably the largest exchange of archer fire ever to take place in the British Isles, would have rained down on the cramped Lancastrian's ranks and caused hundreds, if not thousands, of deaths and woundings within the Lancastrian army.

The Lancastrian assault

The Lancastrian command realised that they could not stand the Yorkist arrow storm for much longer. Clearly, the lighter armoured archers at the front of the Lancastrian ranks were suffering greatly from this exchange of arrow fire, and were instinctively falling back through the Lancastrian ranks to the relative safety of their rear positions. This in turn was greatly unsettling for the Lancastrian army. They could neither wait for the Yorkists to advance upon them, nor stand to wait for the Yorkist archers to finish firing. Fearing that the Lancastrian ranks were about to break, the commanders hurriedly ordered the whole army to advance.

Between 9 and 10 o'clock in the morning, the entire Lancastrian army trudged forward across the 400 hundred or so yards, over their fallen comrades and through hundreds of thousands of spent arrows snow blowing in their faces, towards the waiting Yorkist force across the valley.

We can only imagine the thoughts of the Yorkist soldiers as they watched the Lancastrian army advance towards them. The Yorkist archers withdrew through the ranks to their rear as the Lancastrians marched ever closer, but not before letting loose more volleys into their packed ranks. The men now

in the Yorkist front ranks, who would by now have held a look of either fear or grim determination on their faces, would surely have clasped their weapons even more firmly, as their captains and commanders shouted out words of encouragement to calm any wavering Yorkist nerves, as the soldiers, captains and nobles alike, awaited the Lancastrians and the inevitable final charge towards them over the last few dozen yards.

The initial impact of this charge caused the Yorkist line to give, but it did hold. There commenced several hours of savage hand to hand fighting while soldiers from both sides brought their maces, swords, axes and halberds to bear upon each other.

The main battle

The battle line weaved and buckled at dozens of different locations all along the front, as the stronger on either side crushed their opponents and forced themselves forward ever deeper into the enemy ranks. Edward Hall described the scene on Towton Dale:

> 'The Earl of Northumberland, and Andrew Trollope, which were chieftains of King Henry's vanguard...hastened forwards to join with their enemies: you may be sure the other part nothing retarded, but valiantly fought with the enemies. This battle was sore fought, for hope of life was set on side on every party and the taking of prisoners was proclaimed (before the battle) as a great offence, by reason every man determined to conquer or to die in the field.
>
> 'The deadly battle and bloody conflict continued 10 hours in doubtful victory, the one party some time flowing, and some time ebbing...' [5]

Clearly, the battle was fought in such a manner befitting what was at stake – the very crown of England.

So great was the carnage that at some points along the battle line, it is said that the two sides had to actually stop fighting to clear the bodies that had amassed to their fronts. Once that was done they able to get at each other and continue the melee. It was during one of these occasions that the following event is said to have occurred. Richard Brooke, who visited the battlefield several times, was intrigued by the fate of one Lancastrian noble – Lord Dacre of Gilsland – and wrote:

> 'Persons residing near to the field of battle, readily point out the place where Lord Dacre is said to have been slain, and which I several times made a point of visiting, in the course of my rambles there; it is in a field called North Acres, which seems to have been originally much larger and to have been subdivided...
>
> 'Tradition has it that Lord Dacre was shot at Towton, by a boy "out of a bur tree" and that the place where he was slain is called North Acres, whereupon they have this rhyme, "The Lord of Dacres was slain in North Acres". Others who I conversed with repeated the tradition, and told me that Lord Dacre was slain by an arrow shot by a boy from an Auberry tree, evidently meaning the same shrub that is called a bur tree.' [6]

Lord Dacre retired from the front to to refresh himself, and likely to converse with some of the other Lancastrian commanders. We should not be surprised at this, as it would not take long, (even on a cold winter's day like this one) for a man in heavy armour to grow tired, hot and thirsty and require for liquid refreshment.

In order to take his repast, Lord Dacre removed his helmet and, whilst in the act of drinking, was targetted by the boy. The lad, armed with a crossbow, very quickly got off an extremely competent shot over the heads of the struggling combatants. The arrow plunged into Lord Dacre's neck sending him crashing to the ground where he quickly expired.

(Local tradition has it that the descendant of the bur tree is growing on the site to this day.)

Throughout this sustained Lancastrian assault, Edward, commanding the Yorkist reserve, is said to have continually travelled up and down the Yorkist line throwing himself into battle where the line looked like giving way. Edward, would have certainly been an impressive sight. Dressed in full armour and standing at a height of more than six feet, the presence of the young king, (who was 19 years and one month to the day) at a critical moment accompanied by his household men, would have done much to raise any flagging Yorkist spirits. Surprisingly, of the Earl of Warwick's activity in the battle at this point, the chroniclers are silent.

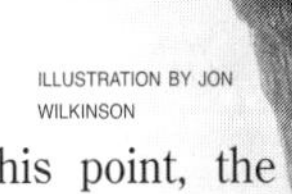

ILLUSTRATION BY JON WILKINSON

The Ambush from Castle Hill Wood and the Yorkist retreat

Slightly after midday, when the two sides had been in combat for approximately three hours, several hundred Lancastrian soldiers suddenly emerged from Castle Hill Wood, where they had been concealed. The wood was on the Yorkist's left flank. It appears that the unknown commander of this Lancastrian ambushing force concluded that the time was ripe to attack. They charged out of cover and smashed into the rear of the Yorkist left flank.

The battle line had not been maintained in a straight line across the whole front, for there is evidence to suggest that the Lancastrian assault – from the very outset was not fully co-ordinated. As a result the Lancastrian right flank was quicker to march and engage with the Yorkists than the Lancastrian left flank. Jean de Waurin wrote that:

> 'When Lord Rivers, his son and six or seven thousand Welshmen led by Andrew Trollope, following the Duke of Somerset himself with seven thousand men, charged his cavalry who fled and were chased for about eleven miles.
>
> 'It seems that Lord River's troops had won a great battle, because they thought that the Earl of Northumberland had charged on the other side, unfortunately he had not done so...'

Thus the activity on the Lancastrian right flank was completely separate to the activity on the left flank. Indeed, the Lancastrians commanding the right flank believed that they had won a victory. The ambush from Castle Hill Wood contributed to the Yorkist left flank giving way to some significant degree.

In the early afternoon the outnumbered Yorkist forces began to give ground to the Lancastrians all along their line. Indeed, it is said that Edward had to commit the reserve to the melee at this point to stop the Yorkist line from collapsing altogether.

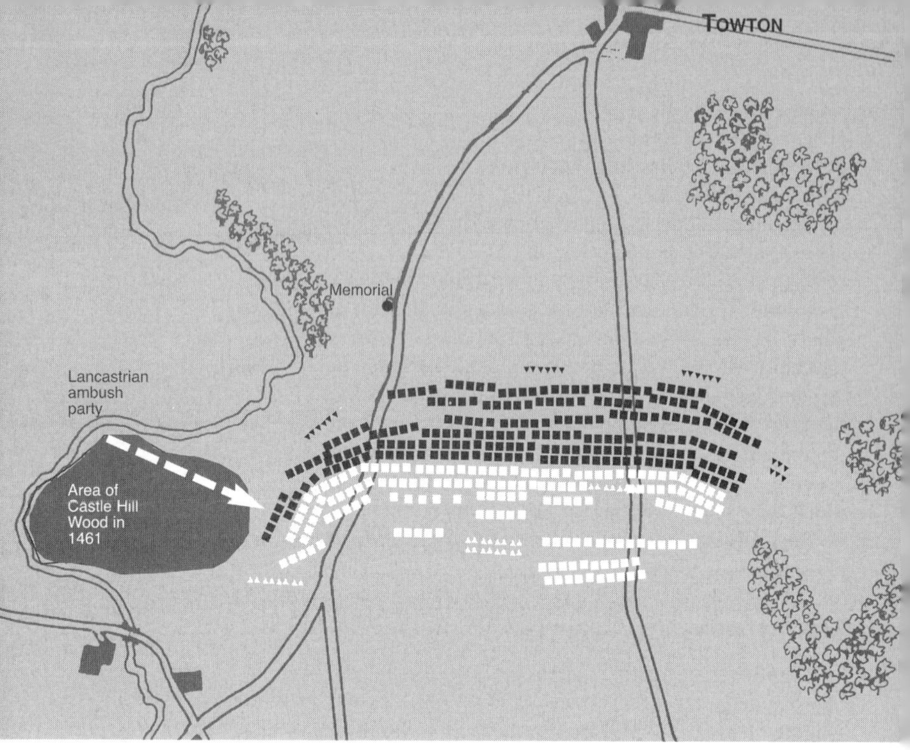

Superior numbers began to tell and the Lancastrians began to turn the Yorkist line by Castle Hill Wood where they had sprung a successful ambush.

Inexorably the Yorkists were pushed back towards the southern most point of the raised plateau over which they had marched to face the Lancastrians that morning.

The arrival of the Duke of Norfolk

Around 4 o'clock, it seems that the Yorkist cause was doomed and that the inevitable break in the Yorkist line and subsequent rout and destruction of the Yorkist army would soon follow. At this moment of pending despair for the Yorkist commanders, it seems their prayers were answered by the final arrival of the Duke of Norfolk and a force of some 5,000 soldiers gathered from East Anglia. In the account of the Wars of the Roses, known as *Hearne's Fragment*, the following is written:

> '...the forsaid John Duke of Norfolk, with a fresh band of good men of war came in, to the aid of the new elected King Edward...' [8]

The ageing Duke of Norfolk had taken so long a time to make an appearance because he was ill, and that his force moved only as fast as the duke's own ageing and sick body would allow them to. Indeed, Norfolk himself stopped when he reached Pontefract Castle acknowledging that he was slowing up the march. Hearing that the Yorkists were already committed to battle, and in order to ensure that his force arrived as quickly as possible on the battlefield, he passed over command to his cousin, Sir John Howard.

Their arrival (along what is now the A162) on the eastern side of the battlefield and their committal to the melee at that point had dramatic impact. At once the Lancastrian left flank began to give way. This partial collapse of their front, and the earlier Lancastrian success on their right flank had totally altered the facing of their line from the one they had held at the start of the battle, a circumstance which was to have significant consequences for the Lancastrians in the latter stages of the battle. Even though they were tired from their day's march, Norfolk's troops were not battle weary. With their assistance Edward's and the Yorkist's fortunes began to change. Slowly they began to gain the upper hand and it was the Lancastrians who now found that they were being pushed back.

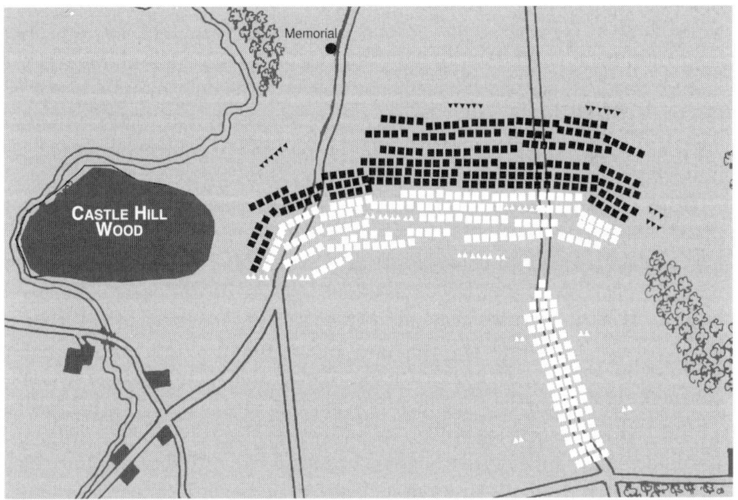

The arrival of the Duke of Norfolk's men at about 4 o'clock in the afternoon had a profound effect on the outcome of the battle.

The Lancastrian rout

The arrival of fresh troops had a positive impact on Yorkist morale, and equally, a negative one on the Lancastrians. Before long, slowly at first, the Lancastrian soldiers began to lose heart and in ever increasing numbers, groups of them began to break ranks and flee the battlefield. The Lancastrians found themselves being pushed back further and further as the Yorkists steadily but surely began to overwhelm them. The situation on the Lancastrian right flank was growing particularly precarious as they realised that they were being pushed closer and closer to the steep banks that led down to the River Cock.

It was the Lancastrian left flank that broke first. The men under the Earl of Northumberland's command, who had taken on the additional burden brought about by the arrival of Norfolk's contingent, suddenly broke.

The collapse on the Lancastrian left flank reverberated along the entire front, and from left to right. At around 5 o'clock in the evening the whole Lancastrian front caved in and thousands of Lancastrian soldiers turned and began running for their lives.

Invariably, the majority of casualties are inflicted upon a defeated enemy force during its rout. This was certainly the case at Towton. Those on the Lancastrian right were to fair the worst. As they turned and fled, they encountered the steep slopes that led down to the River Cock. This steep banking, which is difficult to traverse in even fine and dry weather, was absolutely impossible in the wet and snowy conditions, and they soon began tumbling down its banks into the cold and swollen waters of the River Cock at the base of bank. The cliff edge which they had thought would protect their right flank at the start of the battle, was suddenly their undoing at the battle's close. Those who chose not to traverse the steep banks and who tried to stand their ground, were simply overwhelmed by the more numerous Yorkists and the appalling slaughter in this part of the battlefield was to earn it the name 'Bloody Meadow'.

Those Lancastrians not caught in this slaughter, and who managed to flee the melee (more probably the men on the Lancastrian left flank) headed north hoping to find sanctuary north of Towton and Tadcaster. However, as they converged upon the various crossings over the River Cock and the River Wharfe north of Towton village, they were caught in a series of bottlenecks between the pursuing Yorkists and the swollen waters of the rivers themselves. Many were crushed under foot in the stampede, and as more and more soldiers arrived looking for a place to cross the rivers. Recall that all the bridges had been broken to protect the Lancastrian rear from the possibility of flanking attacks. So great was the crush of bodies that they piled up along the banks of the rivers to such an extent that at several places across these stretches of water it was possible to cross from one side to the other simply by walking over the piled up bodies.

Local tradition states that so great was the slaughter here, that the rivers turned red with blood. There are reports that some of the Lancastrian army, which was pursued all the way into Tadcaster tried unsuccessfully, to make a stand, but again they were over whelmed by the Yorkist forces and slain.

When the Lancastrian line broke Edward had ordered his cavalry to mount their horses and pursue the enemy. He gave the order to 'kill the lords but spare the commoners'. This order to spare the commoners probably fell on deaf ears. The victorious Yorkists mounted and set off in pursuit of the defeated Lancastrians, no doubt encouraged by the thoughts of plunder – particularly of a captain, noble or lord. Previously, both sides had said that no quarter was to be given, and a number of the Lancastrians (such as Sir Andrew Trollope) had a bounty on their heads. These facts alone, further fuelled by the almost over zealous desire for revenge against the Lancastrians. Had they not murdered several prominent nobles during and after the battles of Wakefield and St. Albans? It was they who had allowed their army to plunder and destroy many settlements south of the River Trent in their march south earlier in the year. There were a great many scores to be settled – and now was the Yorkist's time to settle them. Consequently, this pursuit of the defeated enemy lasted well into the evening and most certainly constitutes several of the chronicled ten hours that Edward Hall states the battle lasted.

Edward IV – by the grace of God and by the right of battle – was now

As light began to fail the Lancastrian lines started to disintegrate and groups of men began fleeing northwards towards Tadcaster – the valley of the Cock Beck stood in their way. Many of the Yorkists mounted up and were soon in hot pursuit and a terrible slaughter began.

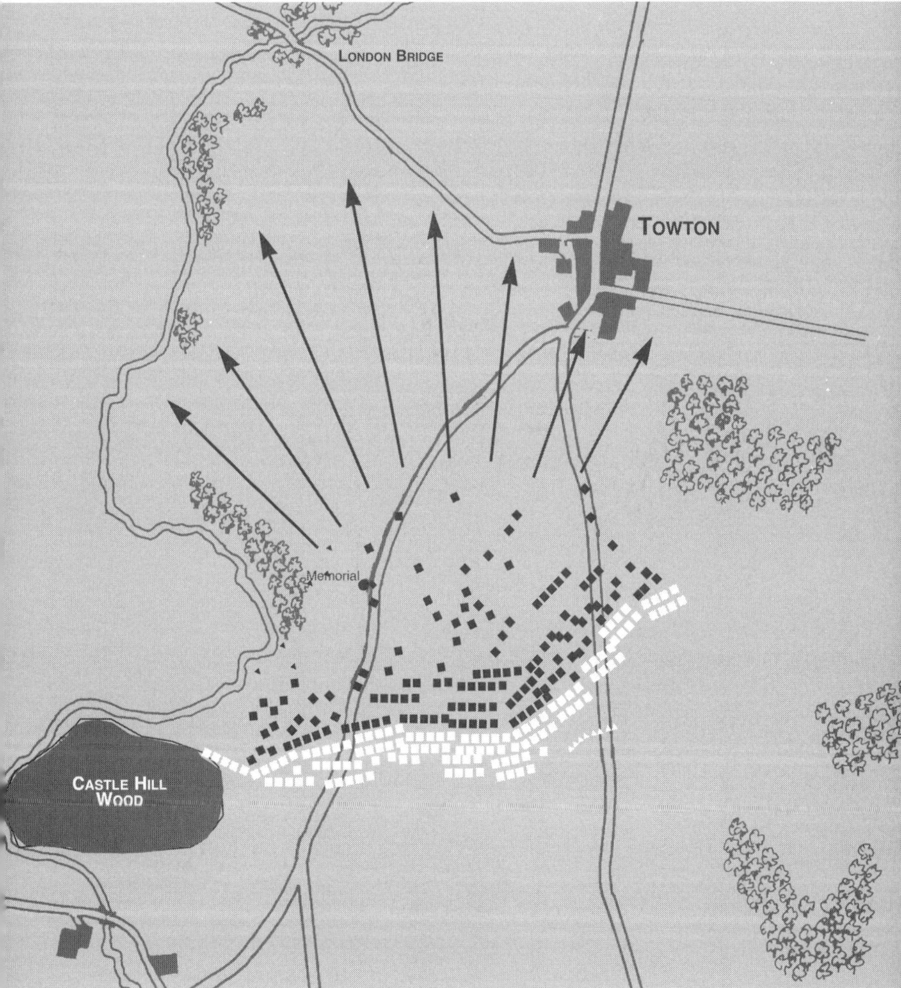

undisputed King of England, and as King of England, he would now bring those who had faced him as his enemies to account for their actions, accounts that many would pay for with their lives.

Aftermath

Not all the Lancastrian nobles who died at the battle of Towton died in the rout. Lord Dacre of Gilsland had died at the hand of a 'sniper' on the field of battle. Also killed during the fighting was the Earl of Northumberland, the Duke of Buckingham, Lord Welles, Lord Willoughby, Lord Mauley and Sir Andrew Trollope. It may have been Northumberland's death on the field that contributed to the collapse of the Lancastrian left flank. In terms of nobles, the Yorkists fared much better. Indeed, the only man of note to die on the battlefield for their cause was Robert Horne.

The Lancastrian commander, the Duke of Somerset and a number of other prominent Lancastrian lords such as the Duke of Exeter, Earl of Wiltshire (who was later captured and executed at Newcastle, his head being taken to London and set on London Bridge), Lord Roos and Sir John Fortescue (the then Chief Justice), managed to survive the rout and escape to York. From there they accompanied the King, Queen and Prince of Wales to safety in Scotland. It has been suggested that these lords realised that the battle was going against them and, before the rout had even begun, left the field and the Lancastrian army to its fate.

After his victory at Towton, Edward travelled to York and arrived there early the following day, with the express hope of capturing King Henry VI, Queen Margaret of Anjou and their son, Edward the Prince of Wales. He arrived too late. Informed of disaster that had befallen their army when the Duke of Somerset had arrived at the city, and now fearing for their own lives, they had fled. A large portion of Edward's army would have

Queen Margaret and King Henry VI. Upon hearing of the defeat and rout of their army at Towton the pair fled from the City of York. Edward IV raced to the city hoping to capture his rivals, but arrived too late.

remained at Towton. The wounded and the dying had to be attended to. The surgeons, with the limited medical knowledge of the times would have been dealing with upper body wounds. Burial parties had to be formed to gather the dead and to dig pits in preparation for mass burials. Salvaging of armour, chained mail, weapons and personal items was carried out by men detailed for that job.

Edward, meanwhile, upon entering the city of York, ordered the removal of the heads of his father, brother and the Earl of Salisbury from above Micklegate Bar, so that they could be reunited with their bodies for formal burial. This would obviate the problem of displaced body parts during the resurrection of the dead – so the belief went. The Yorkists heads would be replaced with prominent Lancastrian ones.

While he was in York he released from captivity Lord Montagu, the Earl of Warwick's brother, who had been captured by the Lancastrians after the 2nd battle of St.Albans. He presided over the trial and execution of some of the lords and nobles captured after the battle. By the end of Monday 30 March, more than forty-two knights, nobles and lords, who had been captured either during the battle or afterwards during the rout, were executed. Edward did spare some of his enemies. Members of the Woodville family, Sir Anthony and Sir Richard, were not only spared, but received pardons. Edward was in love with Elizabeth Woodville and he had a mind to marry in the near future.

Others were not so lucky Thomas Courtnay, Earl of Devon who appears to have been wounded during the battle and taken to York early on Palm Sunday, was to feel the young king's wrath. Gregory wrote in his account of the battle that:

> '...The Earl of Devon was sick in York and could not get away, and was taken and beheaded...' [9]

Devon's was one of the heads to end up on Micklegate Bar. Among the

captured nobility there were found the sons of both Lord Clifford and the Earl of Northumberland, Henry Percy.

Though revenge for the murder of Edward's brother Edmund on Wakefield bridge by John Lord Clifford would have been uppermost on everyone's mind, Edward chose not to revenge himself upon the young Clifford. He spared him, and placed him into the custody of a shepherd in which he remained until restored to his rightful title and lands by Henry VII some twenty years later. As for the young Henry Percy, he was to spend the next nine years as a prisoner in the Tower of London before being restored to his rightful status and regaining the family Earldom of Northumberland. In later years, the earl was to become one of Edward's leading supporters, and later still Richard III's, when Richard claimed the throne in 1483. Percy was later to be blamed for the defeat of the Yorkist army and death of Richard III at Bosworth Field in 1483. He was subsequently murdered at Topcliffe in North Yorkshire in April 1489.

Despite the retributions and executions, it was also a time for reward, and as a direct result of the successful outcome of the battle, Edward made Lord Fauconberg, Earl of Kent. Viscount Bouchier was made Earl of Essex. His brother George was made Duke of Clarence. Knights such as Hastings, Wenlock, Ogle, Herbert and Devereux, who had all served the Yorkist cause well at Towton, St. Albans and Mortimer's Cross were all made lords.

Clearly, the battle of Towton had been a monumental struggle, but what was the cost in human lives? The chroniclers are at odds with each other in regards to the death toll. Hall chronicled that in the whole battle, (including it's rout and the encounters at Ferrybridge and those who died from their wounds in the days and weeks that followed the battle) that some 36,766 men had died. Vergil and Hearne in their respective accounts of the battle both claim 30,000, while in the Croyland chronicle 38,000 men are said to have been killed.

Edward IV himself, in a letter sent to his mother writes that 28,000 men had died. The Paston family, (prolific letter writers of the age) wrote that according to the heralds, (whose role it was after a battle to estimate the numbers of the dead and to identify as many nobles slain in the conflict as possible) 28,000 had died – thus agreeing with Edward. Taking the lowest figure it still means that the battle of Towton has gained a place in history, (and in the *Guinness Book of Records*) for being the largest, longest and bloodiest battle with the single largest loss of life ever to occur on English soil. It must have been a very grim sight to any that surveyed it, and in the *Croyland Chronicle* there is written testament to just how grim:

> '...those who helped inter the bodies piled up in pits and trenches prepared for the purpose, bear witness that eight and thirty thousand warriors fell on that day besides those who drowned in the river whose numbers we have no way of ascertaining. The blood, too, of the slain mingling with the snow which at this time covered the whole surface of the earth, afterwards ran down in the furrows and ditches along the melted snow, in a most shocking manner...' [10]

The consequences of the battle were not lost on the educated people of the age either, and news soon spread of the Yorkist victory. The battle featured in much of the prominent correspondence of the age.

On 7 April 1461, George Neville, (the Earl of Warwick's brother and Bishop of Exeter and Chancellor of England) wrote a letter to Francesco Coppini, the Papal Legate and Bishop of Ternis, in Flanders, that:

> 'There was a great conflict, which began with the rising of the sun, and lasted until the tenth hour of the night, so great was the pertinacity and boldness of the men, who never heeded the possibility of a miserable death. Of the enemy who fled, great numbers were drowned in the river near Tadcaster, eight miles from York, because they themselves had broken the bridge to cut our passage that way, so that none could pass, and a great part of the rest who got away who gathered in the sad town and city, were slain and so many dead bodies were seen as to cover an area six miles long by three broad and about four furlongs. In this battle, eleven lords of the enemy fell, including the Earl of Devon, the earl of Northumberland, Lord Clifford and Neville with some knights, and from what we hear from persons worthy of confidence, some 28,000 persons perished on the one side and the other. O miserable and luckless race...' [11]

It is clear from the letter above – and from countless others – what actually happened on the battlefield at Towton and afterwards, and modern historians should hold them dear for allowing us an invaluable insight into what transpired, thus allowing the story to be retold in our modern age. Although it was a significant victory for the Yorkists, the Wars of the Roses would continue for almost another thirty years. The Lancastrians never really recovered from their defeat at Towton, although many of them continued the cause, most notably the Duke of Somerset who spent the following years in Northumberland organising resistance against the Yorkists on Henry VI's behalf.

As for Edward, he stayed in the north of England for only a short time, and after spending Easter at York, he returned to London and set to the task of running the country. It was to be left to the Earl of Warwick, Lord Fauconberg and the newly released Lord Montagu to seek out the remaining Lancastrians, and what followed was a protracted siege war in Northumberland culminating with the next two battles of the Wars of the Roses at Hexham 1462 and at Hedgeley Moor in 1464. It was only after the successful conclusion of these campaigns – for the Yorkists – that Edward could truly claim that his throne was secure.

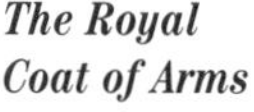

The Royal Coat of Arms

Chapter Seven

Wakefield-Towton History Trail

Whilst the tour really begins at the ruins of Sandal Castle, Wakefield, much may be gleaned from a visit to Richard of York's former property at Conisbrough, just twenty miles from Sandal, and less than ten miles from the A1 (the former Great North Road). On their marches north to do battle with the Lancastrians, gathered at Pontefract Castle, both Richard, and three months later his son Edward, used the Great North Road and, although not recorded, would likely have stayed at least overnight, at their stronghold at Conisbrough.

The rooms, in the sympathetically restored Keep, will help the reader sample the atmosphere of mediaeval life of some 550 years ago. Certainly the newly acclaimed young king, Edward IV, would have warmed himself at the two huge fireplaces; prayed in the castle chapel that God would bless his campaign to wreak vengence on those who murdered his father and brother; used the upper chamber for a review of the situation following the long march from London, and planned with his lords and captains concerning the coming battle (Towton). Yes, and he would certainly have taken the passage off the Lord's Hall and made use of the stone seat over the 'long drop'. Period ambience is guaranteed within the fabric of this excellent castle.

After getting into the right frame of mind at Conisbrough – maybe reading one of the recorded speeches of the period (see page 35), take the A6023 towards Mexborough. Pass Wombwell on the A633 towards Barnsley and carry on to Monk Bretton passing the ruins of Monk Bretton Priory, founded in the 12th Century, and the monks' watermill dating from that time, which has been beautifully restored and now serves as a restaurant – 'The Mill of the Black Monks'.

Proceed to the A61 and on to Sandal Castle, where the outline of its buildings and walls may still be seen. It fell victim to the attentions of Oliver Cromwell – a fate escaped by its twin stronghold at Conisbrough, hence the suggestion to visit Conisbrough Castle at the outset of this tour.

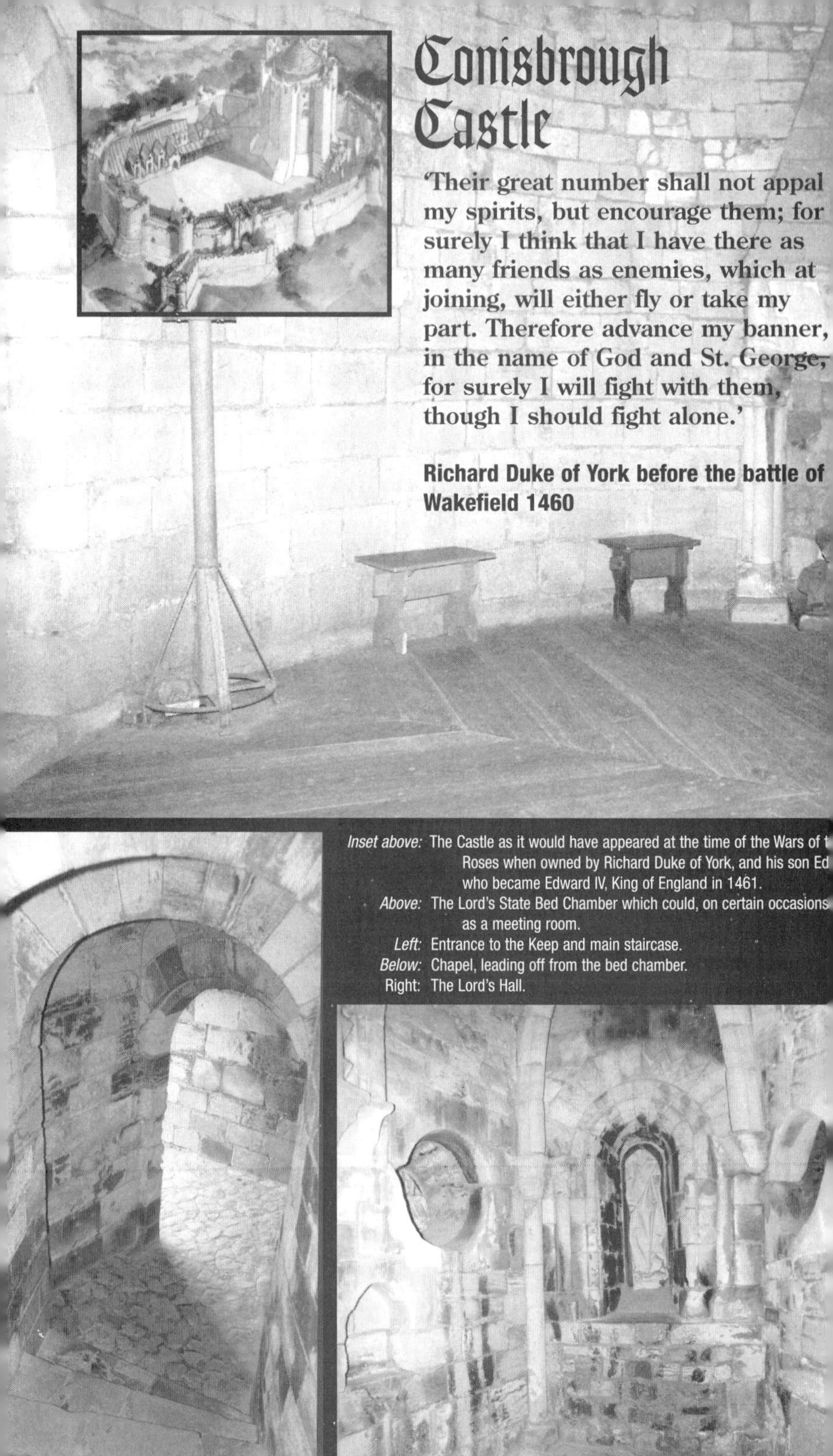

Conisbrough Castle

'Their great number shall not appal my spirits, but encourage them; for surely I think that I have there as many friends as enemies, which at joining, will either fly or take my part. Therefore advance my banner, in the name of God and St. George, for surely I will fight with them, though I should fight alone.'

Richard Duke of York before the battle of Wakefield 1460

Inset above: The Castle as it would have appeared at the time of the Wars of t Roses when owned by Richard Duke of York, and his son Ed who became Edward IV, King of England in 1461.
Above: The Lord's State Bed Chamber which could, on certain occasions as a meeting room.
Left: Entrance to the Keep and main staircase.
Below: Chapel, leading off from the bed chamber.
Right: The Lord's Hall.

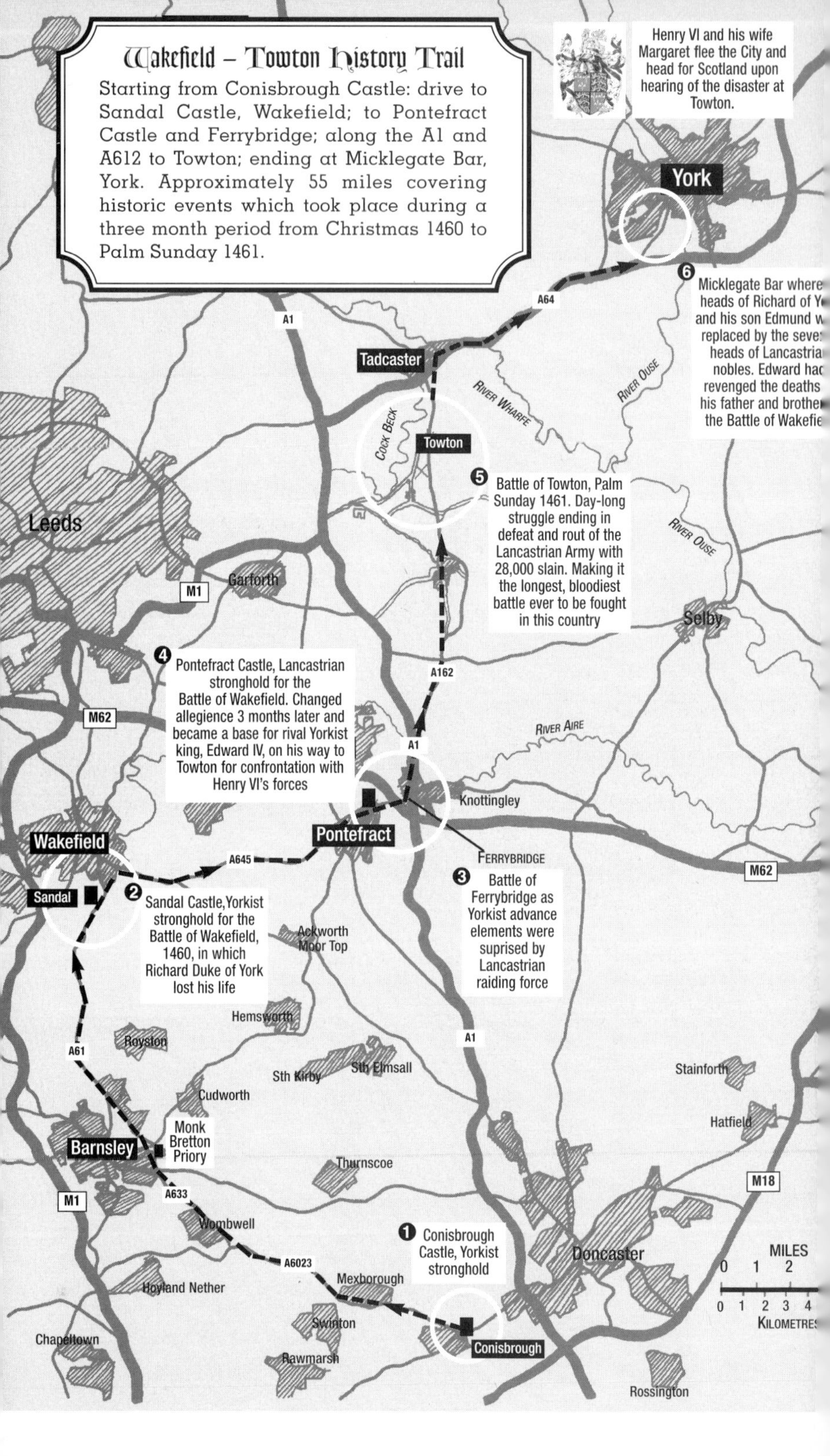

Wakefield – Towton History Trail
Starting from Conisbrough Castle: drive to Sandal Castle, Wakefield; to Pontefract Castle and Ferrybridge; along the A1 and A612 to Towton; ending at Micklegate Bar, York. Approximately 55 miles covering historic events which took place during a three month period from Christmas 1460 to Palm Sunday 1461.
Henry VI and his wife Margaret flee the City and head for Scotland upon hearing of the disaster at Towton.
York
6 Micklegate Bar where heads of Richard of Y and his son Edmund w replaced by the seve heads of Lancastria nobles. Edward had revenged the deaths his father and brothe the Battle of Wakefie
A64
A1
Tadcaster
River Ouse
River Wharfe
Cock Beck
Towton
5 Battle of Towton, Palm Sunday 1461. Day-long struggle ending in defeat and rout of the Lancastrian Army with 28,000 slain. Making it the longest, bloodiest battle ever to be fought in this country
River Ouse
Leeds
Garforth
M1
Selby
4 Pontefract Castle, Lancastrian stronghold for the Battle of Wakefield. Changed allegience 3 months later and became a base for rival Yorkist king, Edward IV, on his way to Towton for confrontation with Henry VI's forces
A162
M62
River Aire
A1
Knottingley
Wakefield
Pontefract
A645
Ferrybridge
3 Battle of Ferrybridge as Yorkist advance elements were suprised by Lancastrian raiding force
M62
Sandal
2 Sandal Castle, Yorkist stronghold for the Battle of Wakefield, 1460, in which Richard Duke of York lost his life
Ackworth Moor Top
Hemsworth
Royston
A61
A1
Sth Kirby
Sth Elmsall
Stainforth
Cudworth
Hatfield
Barnsley
Monk Bretton Priory
Thurnscoe
M18
M1
A633
Wombwell
1 Conisbrough Castle, Yorkist stronghold
Doncaster
MILES
0 1 2
A6023
Mexborough
Hoyland Nether
0 1 2 3 4
Kilometre
Swinton
Chapeltown
Conisbrough
Rawmarsh
Rossington

EXPLORING THE BATTLEFIELD OF WAKEFIELD

The castle can be easily located near to the M1 Motorway by the Denby Dale turn off, (**junction 39**). Motorists travelling either north or south can clearly see the castle from the motorway. The site itself can be found **off the A61**, Barnsley road, and can be easily accessed by turning onto Manygates Lane, where the lane intersects with the A61. There are adequate car parking facilities on site.

Today, little remains of the battlefield of 1460, and there are only a handful of clues to show the passer-by what actually transpired on that fateful day. The castle is a mere vestige of its former glory, due to the fact that it was utterly destroyed at the end of the English Civil War by the orders of Parliament (1646) after it had finally surrendered in 1645. Much of the building had been destroyed by artillery fire during the siege, and because of this, most of the stonework, (some of which had fallen into the ditches surrounding the castle), along with any other recyclable materials, was removed in subsequent years.

Sandal Castle drawn from an Elizabethan painting (see page 37).

In recent years, housing, commercial developments and a park have all but covered what was known as Sandal Common. However, a very small portion of it, later known as Wakefield Green, still remains.

Excavations at Sandal Castle

Between the years 1964 and 1973, a partnership between Wakefield City Council, Wakefield Historical Society and the University of Leeds, under the direction of Phil Mayes and Lawrence Butler, commenced the excavation of Sandal Castle. What is visible today is a testament to the painstaking work carried out by these organisations. The results of this recent excavation are too far reaching and numerous in

The Barbican after excavation looking east. BY COURTESY OF WAKEFIELD HISTORICAL PUBLICATIONS

The Barbican after excavation looking east. BY COURTESY OF WAKEFIELD HISTORICAL PUBLICATIONS

length to be recounted here. For a full analysis read, *Sandal Castle – Wakefield*, by Lawrence Butler, published in 1991 by Wakefield Historical Publications – any exploration of the battlefield at Sandal, must of course start at Sandal Castle itself.

THE TOUR (consult map on page 103)

Locate the remains of the gates and recall that over that very ground, sometime between the 21 and 24 December 1460, Richard Plantagenet, Duke of York entered for the last time.

See Chapter Three, page 31

From the high point afforded by the castle mound, if we look in a northerly direction, the view of what was the battlefield is totally obscured by a housing and commercial development, which today makes up two of the suburbs of Wakefield, the first called Portobello and the later Belle Vue, or as it is sometimes called Belle Isle.

Within the castle, and to the south-east, is an unusual orange segment shaped depression. This depression was a later addition to the defences and was a redoubt, built to help defend the castle in the English Civil War and, at that time would have been able to house several pieces of ordnance. Although in the later excavations no evidence was found to suggest that the defenders of the castle actually had any.

Nothing now remains of the vast stretches of woodland which used to lay to the east and west of Sandal Castle. Today, because of this, and because of housing development, it takes a vivid imagination to bring to mind the view that the Duke of York would have seen, from the same spot, in December 1460.

Cock and Bottle Lane

Having viewed the battlefield from the vantage point of the castle mound and grounds, leave by the car park and proceed down **Manygates Lane**, towards the city of Wakefield. After a short walk along the narrow road which now forms the lane itself, and is enclosed on either side by modern housing, you will come to a residential nursing home, Castle Mount.

Looking along Cock and Bottle Lane.

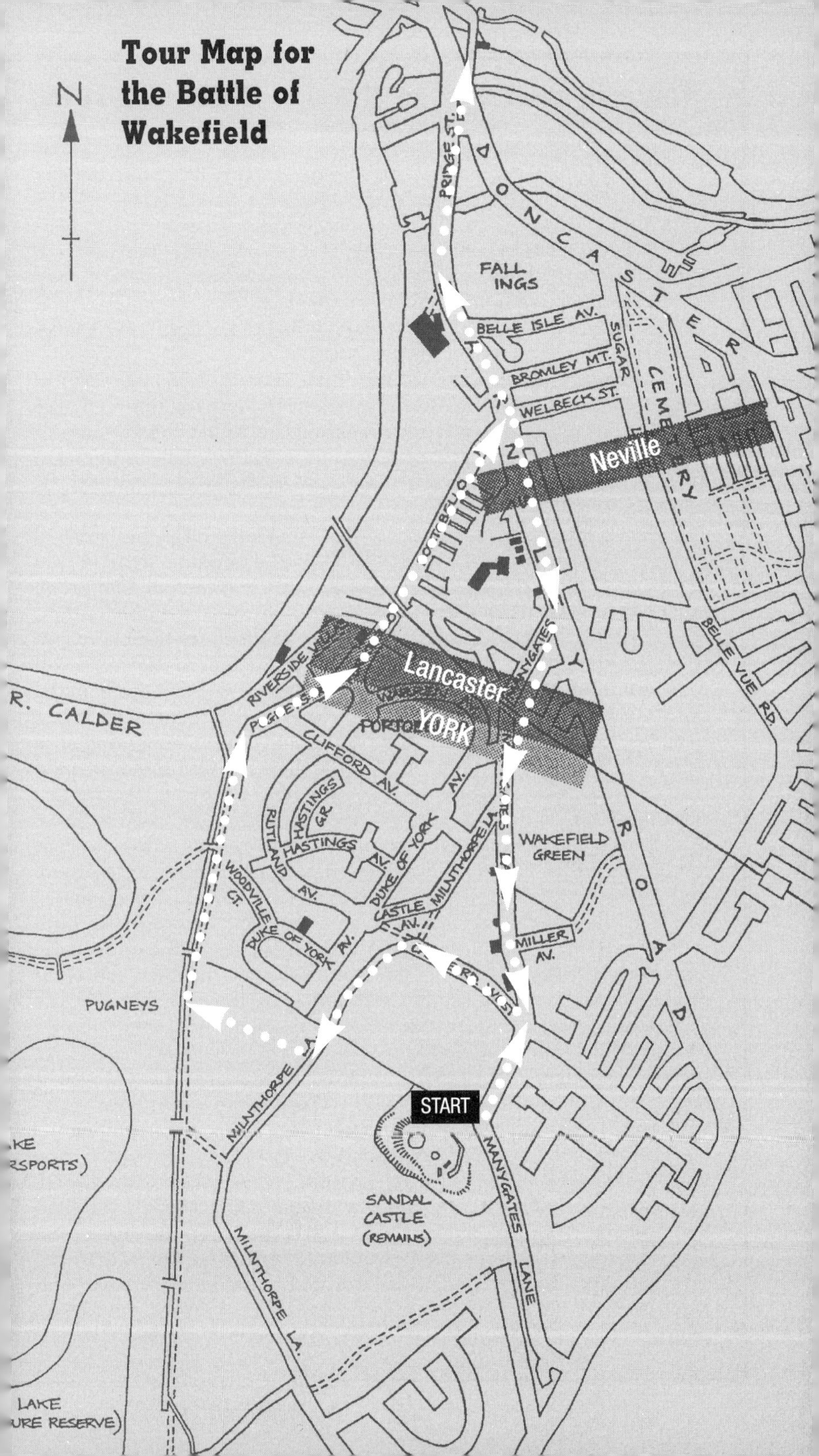
Tour Map for the Battle of Wakefield
N
DONCASTER ROAD
FALL INGS
BELLE ISLE AV.
BROMLEY MT.
WELBECK ST.
SUGAR
CEMETERY
Neville
Lancaster
YORK
R. CALDER
RIVERSIDE
CLIFFORD AV.
HASTINGS GR.
HASTINGS AV.
RUTLAND AV.
DUKE OF YORK AV.
WOODVILLE CT.
CASTLE MILNTHORPE LA.
MANYGATES
WAKEFIELD GREEN
MILLER AV.
BELLE VUE RD.
PUGNEYS
START
SANDAL CASTLE (REMAINS)
MANYGATES LANE
MILNTHORPE LA.

Visits to the Fields of Battle – Wakefield 1856
by Richard Brooke

Richard Brooke visited the battlefields in the 1850s before the site at Wakefield was developed (Towton remains much the same). His work titled, *Visits to the Fields of Battle*, John Russell Smith, 1857, contains a full geographical description of the battlefield before it was built over in the twentieth century, with regards to the location of the battle made the following observations:

'On the 31st of July, 1852, I first visited the field of battle, the castle, and also the village and church of Sandal...

'...looking from Sandal Castle Hill, a flat plain appears, of considerable extent, cultivated as meadow fields, extending from the castle to the river Calder. These meadows are called 'the Pugnays'...

'...adjoining the tract of meadow land is 'Porto – Bello' a mansion erected by Samuel Holdsworth, Esq., and now occupied by William Shaw, Esq...

'...The battle was fought upon that spot and upon the tract of ground formerly part of Wakefield Green, extending from thence across the turnpike road in a north-eastwardly direction. The green must have been on the southward side of the river, and about half a mile from the bridge; its site is crossed by the modern turnpike road, from Wakefield to Barnsley, and part of it has acquired the name Fall Ings, according to tradition, from great numbers who fell there, in the battle. There are now no remains of Wakefield Green, all of it has been enclosed, and several portions of it are built upon; and it is worthy of notice, that on the one side of the spot, where the green is said to have been, the ground descends from Sandal to the present turnpike road, and on a tract of level ground close to Porto Bello House; and that, at a little distance further on the turnpike road leading towards Wakefield, there is a slight elevation in the road, and in the contiguous fields. After carefully viewing the ground, I came to the conclusion that this elevation, which faces the high ground at Sandal, must be considered to have been the position of the Lancastrians; and also that the battle was fought upon the level ground between it and Sandal, extending on the one side towards Porto Bello House, and on the other to the Fall Ings, and towards Pontefract Road. In digging the foundations of Porto Bello House, and in forming the sunk fence there, human bones, broken swords, spurs, and other relics, were discovered, which were considered fully confirmatory of that locality having been the scene of the conflict. On the northern part of Fall Ings, near the side where the highway to Pontefract runs, fragments of armour, and other indications, apparently of the battle, are said to have been discovered some time ago, in making an excavation there. It was also the spot, and on the side of Sandal, where the battle would naturally take place, after the advance of the Lancastrians from York [Pontefract] to Wakefield; and it tallies with the accounts handed down to us, that the battle was fought between Wakefield and Sandal, and upon Wakefield Green.'

Before reaching this spot, on the left hand side of the road between the nursing home and Castle Road West – there can be found a short **row of terraced houses**. These buildings were, before being converted to residential accommodation, joined together, and formed the Cock and Bottle public house. Manygates Lane was originally called after this public house, and therefore was, for many years, known as 'Cock and Bottle Lane'.

This site is also the birth place of George Scholry who was born in 1758, and who was in later life, Lord Mayor of London and Alderman of that city. Scholry was a local benefactor – and who after making his wealth as a merchant and by marriage, left £10,000 to the poor of Wakefield upon his death.

The Inn was a stopping place for coaches using the turnpike road and became a residential block after losing its licence as an inn during 1866.

Once the Cock and Bottle public house and now a private house.

The battlefield

The aforementioned Castle Road West, is situated on the left hand side of the road before the nursing home. While walking down Manygates Lane, in the direction of Wakefield, upon reaching this road, turn west (**to the left**) and follow this road, which, after a small distance becomes a 'dirt' track, until you reach the open ground just after the houses located on the right hand side. From this spot we are able to view what I believe is the battlefield – albeit covered with modern day housing. However, this spot offers a good opportunity to view how steep the gradient is from Sandal Castle down towards what would have been Wakefield Green.

Having viewed this sight, **continue along this road** as it circumnavigates the open ground previously seen from the castle, (which can be viewed to the left). When this road straightens out from the bend into Milnthorpe Lane, which very closely follows the route of the old mediaeval road to Wakefield, and when we have reached the end of the built up area (to the right), **take the footpath** leading off to the west (**right**), which is present at that point and walk down towards the river, on the footpath which is situated between the field and the housing estate.

Portobello House

When the footpath cuts to the dirt road – at the point where the footpath meets the brick bridge over the drain – turn north (**right**), and walk parallel to the river until you reach the open grassland found to the left, just prior to the housing estate. The road leading off from this point is Pugneys Road. A further walk of some **fifty yards** will lead to the opening of **Riverside Villas**. It was between this point, and the Portobello public house, some fifty yards further along Pugneys Road where it joins with Portobello Road, where the site of the house and gardens of Portobello House once stood.

In building this house, in 1825, various artefacts were discovered, that are said to be connected with the battle. Of these finds, none remain to be viewed by the modern historian. Only one is said to survive, which was found near to the site of Portobello House, and that is a sword, alleged to have been found on a location to the south of the house itself.

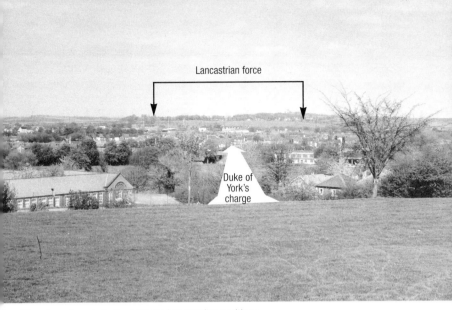

View from the castle towards the Lancastrian positions.

Looking towards Sandal Castle mound from the Lancastrian positions.

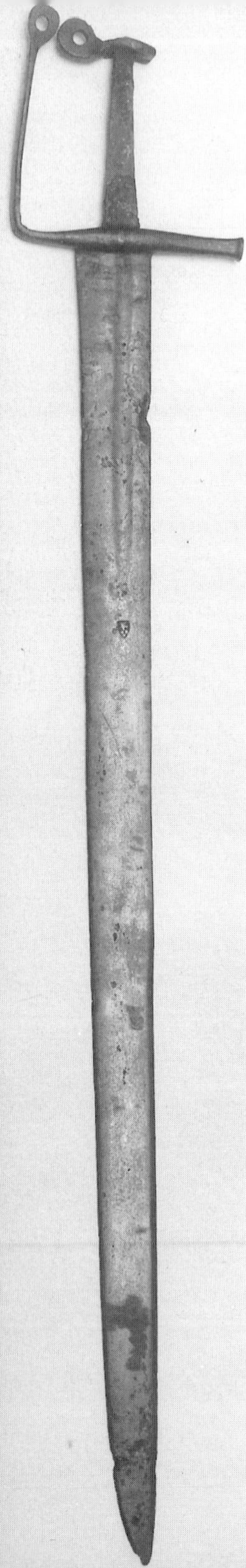

Little is known of this sword, and after its sale at Christies in April 1966 its location was lost, as the buyer wished to remain anonymous. Previous to this sale, it was in the collection of H.C. Haldane, of Clarke Hall, who wrote that the sword was:

'...dug up a few years ago during the operation of cutting a main drain near the site of the battle of Wakefield...' [1]

Richard Knowles wrote that the sword:

'..is of unusual sort, not a knightly weapon, but single edged, possibly cut down from a larger blade. It has a curious guard with an extension of the cross guard protecting the back of the hand. Whilst this is a late medieval form, some concern may be felt that this particular type of sword has tended to be dated by the Wakefield example despite its rather doubtful provenance.' [2]

Nothing at all remains of 'Portobello House' and its surrounding gardens, but its site is significant in determining the proximity of where the battle was fought.

Towards Wakefield Bridge

If we leave this estate behind us, and continue our **walk down Portobello Road** which eventually merges with the A61 – or as it used to be called – the Barnsley turnpike road. Continue towards the centre of Wakefield using the **old Wakefield Bridge** over the Calder. The bridge marks the alleged location of the death of Richard of York's son, the young Earl of Rutland.

While travelling towards the bridge, where Portobello road meets the A61, you will pass on the left hand side of the road the bus station. It is in this location that the Lancastrian right flank at the start of the battle was situated. Almost opposite is the turning into Belle Vue Avenue,

Sword discovered in 1825 when digging a drain in the vicinity of the castle. It was sold at Christies in 1966 and its whereabouts are no longer known.

The east side of the bridge dates from the mediaeval period and the arch construction does not match the 'upstream' side, where bridge widening has taken place. GW

and a little to the south of this are the turnings into Bromley Mount and Welbeck Street. It is in a line, cutting through these roads that the Lancastrian front extended towards the cemetery, which lies to the east of Sugar Lane.

The Bridge and Chapel

Shortly afterwards you will come to the bridge, and the chapel built upon it. We are fortunate in having the very detailed work of Dr John Walker to consult, when considering its history. His study remains an authoritative work even today. In recounting the chapel's history he wrote:

> 'The idea that the chapel was built after the battle of Wakefield, by Edward IV, that the masses might be said for the souls of those who fell in the fray, especially for his father – the Duke of York – and his brother – the Earl of Rutland, has long held possession in the public's mind, but the impression is a totally erroneous one...
>
> '...We have no knowledge as to when the first bridge was built over the Calder at this place, but on February

18th 1342. Edward III granted the bailiffs of the town of Wakefield tollage for three years on all goods for sale and animals passing over the bridge:

'...as a help towards the repairs and improvements of the said bridge, which is now rent and broken...

'I think it very possible that when the bailiffs of the town examined the bridge and applied for help in 1342, they saw that a new bridge was required and that at this time the suggestion was first made that a chapel in honour of the Blessed Virgin Mary should be erected by the townsfolk, as was done on so many other bridges during this century...

'...if my surmise be correct, that it was about this time that the plans were first discussed, doubtless the period which elapsed before the building was commenced would be spent in collecting funds. The construction of the bridge started soon after 1342, when the right of tollage was granted to the bailiffs...

'There are several proofs showing that the erection and endowment of this bridge-chapel were undertaken and completed by the townsfolk of Wakefield. The guilds of the town probably contributed freely to this work, stimulated by the priests who served at the various chantry-altars in their parish church, two of whom – William Bull and William Kay – were among those who applied for the king's licence in 1357.

'The basement of the chapel was undoubtedly built at the same time as the bridge, for the masonry of the two is bonded together, and the walls of the chapel and the piers of the bridge are constructed of the same sandstone...' [3]

It appears that the building of the bridge and chapel was delayed, as Wakefield, like many of the other towns of the country, recovered from the ravages of the Black Death. However, the chapel was completed, and was being serviced by two resident chaplains by 1357. In his paper on the history of the chapel, Walker devotes much of his work to the day to day running of the chantry and gives details of many of the events that occurred, over the years, in the colourful history of the chapel. The following extract gives an account of the later history of the chapel and tells how it fell into disuse:

'When in 1534, Henry VIII sent commissioners

The chapel as it appeared during the 17th Century

The mediaeval chapel facade was replaced in Victorian times. It was rebuilt in the grounds of Kettlethorpe Hall, and later dismantled and put into storage. It was in front of this edifice that Edmund, Earl of Rutland, was put to death by 'Butcher' Clifford, in 1460.
BARNSLEY LIBRARIES, ARCHIVES & LOCAL STUDIES DEPARTMENT

throughout the kingdom to compile the Valor Ecclesiasticus, in order that he might know the value of his first-fruits of all benefices, the chantry in this chapel was returned as an annual value of £12 8s. 11d and the two priests Richard Seal and Tristram Harton, had each an income of £6 3s. 7d. The Act for the dissolution of chantries was passed in the 37th year of the reign of Henry VIII. (1545)...

The chapel then passed into several 'private' hands until it was:

> '...conveyed to the trustees of the general poor of Wakefield, now known as the governors of the charities; but the deed making it over to them was probably lost when the Parliamentarian soldiers under Sir Thomas Fairfax broke into the room over the south porch of the parish church, after the capture of Wakefield on Whit-Sunday morning, May 21st 1643 and destroyed many of the papers kept there by the governors.
>
> 'The trustees of the general poor of Wakefield [the governors] let out the Chapel to various tenants...' [4]

From this point in time, it appears that the chapel was used for many different types of commercial venture; warehousing, clothes dealers, corn factor's office and a cheese makers are all amongst those who made use of the key trading location that the bridge could offer. It was only in the mid 1800s, that a serious attempt was made to reinstate the chapel as a place of religious worship.

Wakefield Green

Once the bridge and chapel have been viewed then we should begin to **retrace the steps** we have taken in reaching this point. We should note however, that as we return towards Manygates Lane, that the area of Wakefield we are now walking upon, was that which was remarked by Brooke as being called the 'Fall Ings'. Brooke, in his visit to Wakefield in 1852 remarked that:

> '...it has acquired the name Fall Ings, according to tradition, from great numbers who fell there, in the battle...' [5]

This is probably the scene of where the Lancastrians caught up with many of the fleeing ranks of the Yorkist troops, during the rout. It is likely that many Yorkists died here, as they tried to make the crossing over the Calder at the bridge, having been caught in the open ground just before it. As we move on, and in retracing our steps, upon reaching Portobello Road, instead of turning down that road towards the site of 'Portobello House', **continue along the A61** until we reach Manygates Lane. **Turn onto the Lane** and continue along it, until we have travelled under the railway bridge. At that point, what remains of Wakefield Green will shortly come into view on the left hand side of the road. Although much of this area is surrounded by the grey of suburbia, including a school, it is only at this point that the first physical clue, to show that the battle took place, comes into view.

If one looks closely at the boundary wall of the school to the right of Manygates Lane as we walk towards the castle, there can be found, hiding under the umbrella of foliage from the surrounding trees and shrubs, an iron railing enclosure. Within this – which actually marks the spot where Edward IV first installed a memorial to his father's death – there can be found a stone monument, erected in 1897, to replace the original cross destroyed in the

THE ABSENCE OF GRAVE PITS

The battle of Wakefield is a conundrum in many ways. Indeed, even the site of the battlefield itself leaves many unanswered questions. Chief amongst these, is, in the absence of any grave pits upon the field of battle, an indication as to where those who were slain in the battle are buried. Brooke, who was afforded the opportunity to view the battlefield before twentieth century developments destroyed it forever:

'There has not been discovered, within the memory of man, any large trench or pit near Sandal Church, where it might reasonably be supposed that some of the slain would be interred, such as has been discovered at Battlefield Church, in consequence of the battle of Shrewsbury, and at Saxton Church, in consequence of the battle of Towton.'

However, there is some reason to believe that there were burials carried out close to where Portobello House once stood. On the Ordinance Survey map of the 1850s, the site of Portobello House is partially enclosed by the loop of a contour which runs from that point – east before the castle – on towards Sandal itself. From a point east of the castle looking west towards that area is a natural dip in the ground (the housing estate hinders the view). It is possible that a part of this natural feature was used to collect together the dead bodies, and that they are buried beneath the open ground to the south of where the housing estate has been built, towards the river.

It is only at this location, on the site of where Portobello House once stood, that any remains – in the form of bones, artefacts and weapons – are said to have been found. Other than debris of war, discovered in the Fall Ings and east of the Barnsley to Wakefield Road, there is no other evidence, at this time, to suggest where the 2,000 plus troops who were killed were laid to rest.

The monument erected in 1897 to commemorate the death in battle of Richard Duke of York. This early photograph gives an idea of how the area appeared prior to building development in the late 1920s. This column stands on the spot of the previous memorial – a wooden cross – which was put up on the orders of King Edward IV, in 1461, to mark the spot where his father, Richard, made his last stand. The original marker was destroyed during the Civil War and siege of Sandal Castle in 1645.

English Civil War when the castle was besieged by the army of Parliament.

In regards to the original cross mentioned above, the *Sandal Castle Report* of 1966 states,

> 'As a memorial, the duke's son, when he ascended the throne as Edward the 4th, erected a cross on the spot where his father fell. The cross stood on the west side of Cock and Bottle lane, a hundred yards beyond the junction of this lane and the one running between the castle and the river to Milnthorpe. This was demolished by the Roundheads in the Civil War but another memorial, in the form of a column (now present) was erected at the same place in 1897. See also Vol. 44 of *English Civil War – Notes and Queries*, (pages 3 – 7).'
>
> 'In this account, reference is made to the forces of Parliament destroying the cross that was erected to commemorate the death of the Duke of York.

'The current monument is about 12' in height and from a point two feet below its pinnacle it is carved with ornate decorations, some of which, have sadly been vandalised. Towards its base is an inscription which reads as follows:

Photograph GW

> 'Richard Plantagenet Duke of York – fighting for the cause of the white rose fell on this spot in the battle of Wakefield December 30th 1460.'

To the right of this, is an endorsement by the people who instructed the monument's erection, it reads as follows:

> 'This stone was erected in 1897 by some who wish to preserve the traditional site.'

Also, upon the monument are four decorative panels on which are engraved the arms and motto of the Duke of York, the Falcon and Fetterlock, the White rose, and Broom (genista), the Plantagenet emblem – from which they took their name. 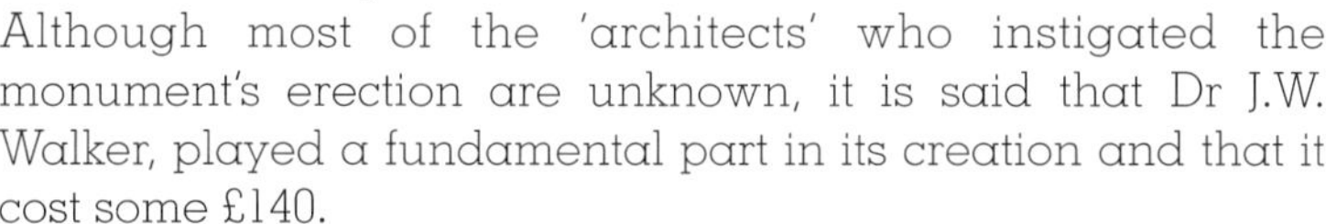
Although most of the 'architects' who instigated the monument's erection are unknown, it is said that Dr J.W. Walker, played a fundamental part in its creation and that it cost some £140.

Despite this inscription on the monument, which claims that this was the spot where the Duke of York made his 'last stand'. I have noted in an old book, – titled *Walks about Wakefield*, by W.S Banks printed in 1871 – an engraving which is said to be from a photograph taken by G. Hall, which shows two willow trees growing on the spot, which is now, the most northerly point, or apex of the triangular piece of ground on which the school is built.

It is possible that these two willow trees, are the ones mentioned by Brooke who visited the spot in 1852, Tyas in 1854 and by Markam in 1886 – when only one tree remained – and could be the true location of the duke's death.

The school building and playground, was built upon the '...triangular piece of ground, with a fence about it...' that Mr Norisson Scatcherd alluded to in the extract. This being the site of the duke's last stand, then it must have been along the route of the Yorkists' fighting retreat back towards the safety of the castle. Consequently, the park opposite, and the school

Where Richard duke of York made his last stand.

playground behind it, where children have played so happily over recent years were, some five hundred and fifty years ago, the scene of great slaughter.

Inevitably, the carnage of the fifteenth century when men's blood soaked the surrounding ground, has given impetuous to local folklore and stories of supernatural happenings. It is said, that, even in recent years, some local inhabitants have commented on 'unusual experiences'. Indeed, a very thoroughly Yorkshire warning, has come down to us, which reads as follows:

'Mind th' Duke o' York, without his head, doesn't git hod o' thi', as tha' gans by th' willo' tree.'

A little above the monument, on the right hand side of the road, before we reach the end of the triangular piece of ground, is the site – though long disappeared – of the well that Brook remarked on.

It is a shame that the well and the Cock and Bottle public house no longer remain. After completing this walk, the walker would surely have appreciated; as I am sure Brooke did after he completed his own exploration of the battlefield, – the refreshment that either would have afforded.

Return to the castle for the next part of the Wakefield-Towton trail. Should you wish to visit Pontefract Castle take the **A645 from Wakefield** (the likely route taken by the Lancastrians in their march to confront Richard of York at Sandal Castle during the last week in December 1460. Or go directly to the site of the action fought at Ferrybridge.

Pontefract Castle (as it appeared 150 years after the Wars of the Roses), although a Lancastrian stronghold, it was used as a base by Yorkist king Edward IV in his advance to do battle north of the River Aire. The custodian of the castle must have changed sides – not an unusual occurrence during the Wars of the Roses.

Beneath the mound that once housed the castle keep steps lead down to a well, across which a plank-walk takes you to a walled-up doorway (*right*). It is believed that five dungeons, dating from the mediaeval period, are located there. If this is correct, then it is more than likely that the Yorkist captives, taken at the Battle Wakefield, were incarcerated here and would have been led up the steps to their execution the next day. This part of the castle is not open to the public at this time. However, the magazine used to hold captives during the Civil War may be visited (*below*).

See Chapter Four, page 55

EXPLORING THE BATTLEFIELD AT FERRYBRIDGE

From Sandal Castle, return to the **M1** and head north at **Junction 39** towards **Leeds**. At the crossing of the **M62 turn east**, (right) following the signs to **Hull** and **Pontefract**. Leave the motorway at **Junction 32** and turn onto the **A639**, sign-posted **Pontefract and Castleford** – be aware of the feeder road that takes you into the retail park.

Travel along the **A639** (also sign-posted A656 to Castleford) – past the Singing Chocker public house on your left – until you reach a small roundabout. At the roundabout **turn right** and follow the **B6136** towards **Ferrybridge**. Travel on this road for a couple of miles – past the The New Airedale public house on your left. As the houses start to fall away you will shortly see the **Ferrybridge power station** come into view and you should keep heading towards it. As you pass the power station (on your left) and go under a railway bridge, look for and take the **left turn immediately** after you pass the large building (on the left behind the trees) which houses the Innogy Technical Support Group. You will see the bridge (which is no longer used by traffic) directly in front of you.

View from the north side of the bridge at Ferrybridge. It was from this bank and this position that Clifford's mounted men, known as 'The Flower of Craven', would have fired volleys of arrows at the Yorkists attempting to repair the section of wooden bridge broken by the Lancastrians.

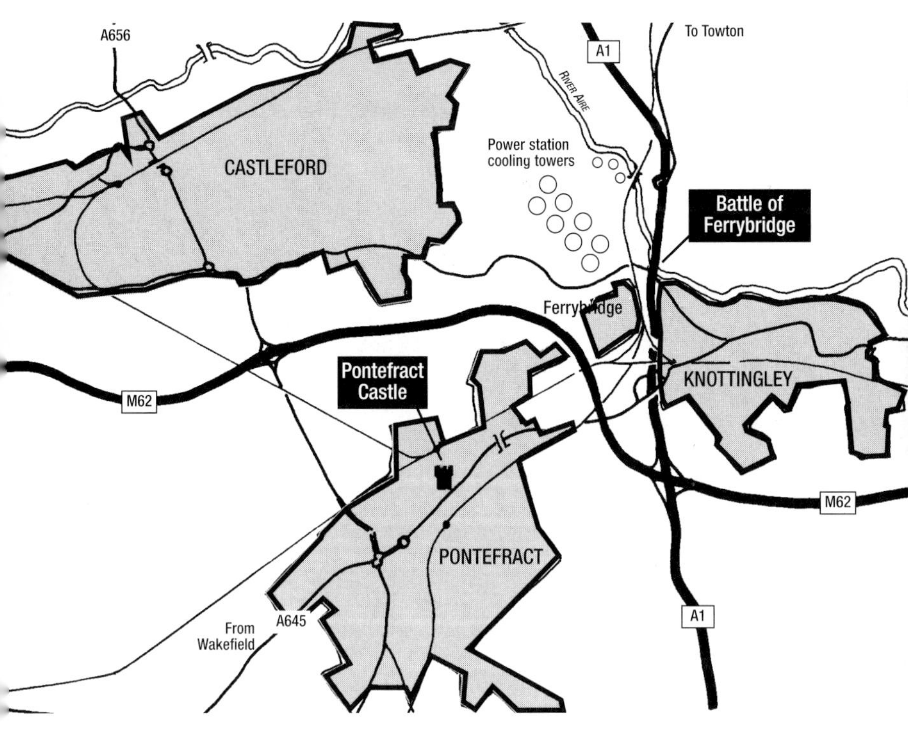

Park up. As you walk to the bridge, look to where you turned in to reach this location, opposite is the road that takes you to the A1 or the Great North Road. It is upon that line of march that the Yorkists would have approached the bridge in their advance from Pontefract Castle, 27th and 28th March 1461, to meet the Lancastrian forces for the momentous showdown.

The Bridge

The bridge that you see before you was completed in 1804, and was, up until the early 1960s, the major crossing of the River Aire for the A1 at this location. The completion of the more modern bridge (to your right as you walk to the old bridge) made the one that you are standing on redundant. When it was in use, the road crossed the river via the bridge and turned sharp left and tapered to join a road that is currently occupied by the modern day A1 – that you can clearly see in front of you – and carried on in a northerly direction.

At the centre of the bridge, set in the walls to either side are monuments to the builders. Again if you are facing the

View from the Yorkists' side, south bank, of the bridge at Ferrybridge.

motorway the one to the left reads: 'John Carr Esquire, of York, Architect 1797'...and the one to the right reads, 'Bernard Hartley, of Pontefract, Builder 1804'.

* * * *

It is difficult to picture in the mind's eye the events of those days – considering the modern day developments that now surround the area. The bridge would have been a wooden structure that stood on or about this location. This then was the vital crossing point that the Yorkists fought valiantly to retake on 28 March 1461.

Although called Ferrybridge, there is evidence to suggest that there was in fact a bridge (and not a ferry) at this location from as early as 1070AD. Indeed, it is said that William the Conqueror crossed at this point as he marched north to suppress the people of Northumberland after the battle of Hastings. During the 14th Century it is recorded that several grants were issued to pay for bridge repairs demonstrating that the crossing here was of importance for maintaining commerce both north and south of the river.

As such, we should not be surprised to learn that the engagement fought here in 1461 was not the last. Clearly, the crossing of the River Aire at this point was an important strategic location as well as an important commercial one. In the year 1644, during the English Civil War, the bridge and surrounding areas to the north were held by the forces of Parliament under the command of a Colonel Sands against an attacking force of Royalists who also tried to force a crossing here.

Brotherton Marsh

Returning to the modern day, again if you stand in the middle of the bridge facing the motorway, the village that you can see to the left is Brotherton. As you look towards the village you can clearly see the church tower. A local historian named Forrest, wrote in a work titled, *The History of Knottingly*, about local speculation regarding the resting place of at least one Yorkist noble who died in the battle and that:

> '...there was found in digging a grave in Brotherton churchyard, May 21st 1781, a chalice, very much mutilated, and it's lid, a spur and parts of armour. These most probably belonged to one of the lords slain at Ferrybridge...
>
> ....it was usual to inter the lords who fell in this contest near the place where they were slain, and it is probable that the chalice, spur and armour might belong to Lord Fitzwalter...' [6]

Unfortunately, none of the above mentioned artefacts appear to have survived to be viewed today, and as such, the story cannot be proved or disproved either way despite the fact that it does appear to have perpetuated itself by becoming a part of local folklore. The open ground between the bridge and the village is known locally as 'little marsh'. Beyond the bridge (in front of you, but obscured by the modern day motorway) is a larger piece of open ground which extends for several miles until you reach the villages of Beal and Burkin which you cannot see from this location, and is known locally as 'big marsh'. Again, Forrest, in his work *The History of Knottingly* writes that:

> '...human skeletons, ancient armour and other relicts of civil warfare have been frequently found there, and should the marsh ever be under the plough, many more such relics will certainly be turned up.' [7]

Although it is an intriguing thought, until such artefacts surface for the modern historian to review and investigate, it is difficult to say whether or not they were remnants belonging either to the mediaeval or the Civil War period.

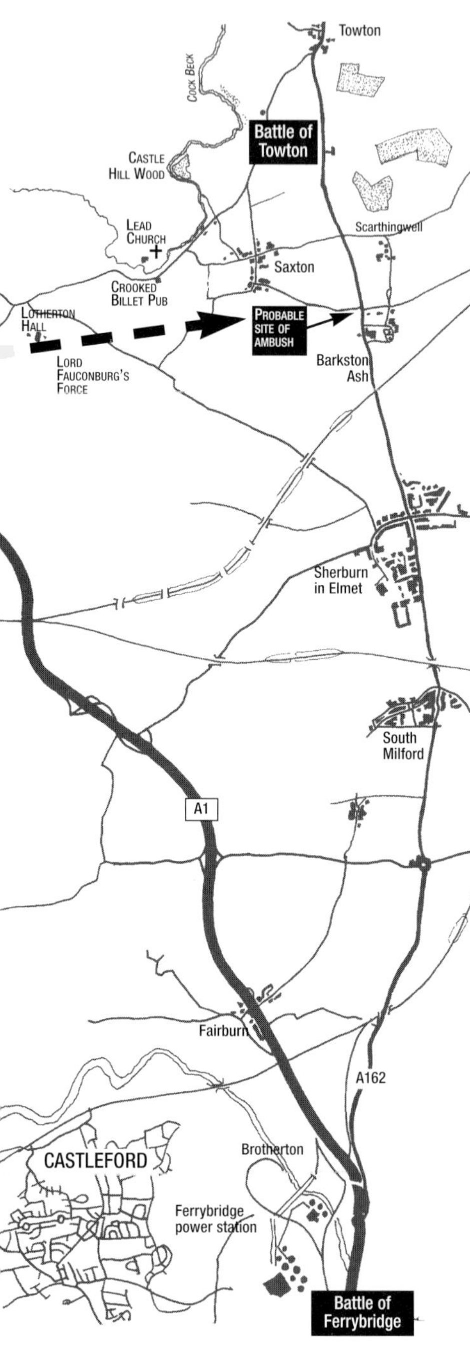

FOLLOWING THE YORKISTS TO THE BATTLEFIELD AT TOWTON

Having reviewed the bridge and the surrounding areas, we can then proceed to the Towton battlefield.

At this point we have two choices. Wc can, (as much as modern-day roads allow us) follow the route that Edward would have taken, or alternatively, the route taken by Fauconberg and possibly a portion of the vanguard. Both routes end at the same place near to Saxton in preparation to explore the battlefield at Towton. The author's recommendation is that the reader should follow the Sherburn-in-Elmet route. The Fauconberg one is included for readers who at some stage, want an alternative route to the battlefield..

The advance of Edward IV via Sherburn-in-Elmet

To follow, (again as best we can) Edward's march, we should leave the bridge and take the access road to the A1 located almost opposite to where you turned in to arrive at the bridge. You can only go northbound if you take this road. **Enter onto the A1**, but be prepared to come off almost immediately. The next junction is to Brotherton, but just past that is another **exit marked A162 Sherburn-in-Elmet**. Be aware that there is an earlier sign which states A63 to Sherburn-in-Elmet, please ignore this. Come off the motorway and the road will rise and go to the right as it crosses the A1 – follow this road towards Sherburn-in-Elmet. As you approach the **mini roundabout, take the 2nd exit** – keeping **The Fox Inn** on your left. Continue along the A162 for several miles, **past Brotherton Quarry** (and over the railway bridge) across the first roundabout (following the sign for Tadcaster and York) until you reach the second roundabout which indicates a **left turn** (which you should take) towards South Milford.

Continue through South Milford (under the railway bridge) still following the signs for Sherburn-in-Elmet (and Tadcaster). Shortly, you will enter into Sherburn-in-Elmet. The road takes you through the centre of the village past **The Red Bear** public house by the light controlled cross-roads. This is the main street, and as you continue along it, consider the English Civil War action that took place many years later, over the ground you are now travelling along as you head towards Barkston Ash.

Barkston Ash, Dintingdale and the death of Lords Clifford and Neville

See Chapter Five, page 73

As you travel to Barkston Ash you come to another **roundabout**, go straight ahead (following the sign to Tadcaster – A162), and shortly you will pass under a bridge before you enter the village. As you pass under this bridge, look behind to the high ground to the left – we will come back to what secret this view could possibly hold shortly.

Continue along the A162 through Barkston Ash, and after some distance, you will come to a **small cross-roads**. At this cross-roads, which can be identified by the large sign that advertises Scarthingwell Golf Club (located on the right), **turn left** and pull in to the passing place on the left hand side of the road. The passing place can hold the length of more than one car and is a good place to stop.

Leave your car and walk back to the cross-roads. If you turn to face the direction of Barkston Ash and look then to the spot between where your car is parked and the road leading

Historians Ken Everitt and Ed Lee at the 'Leper Pot' – an object of curiosity for the battlefield visitor. Does this stone mark the spot where 'Butcher' Clifford was cut down with an arrow in the neck? Some historians believe so. Would the surrounding terrain lend itself to the concealment of Yorkist mounted scouts under the command of Lord Fauconberg? Whichever location, it was a brilliant and audacious action carried out under the very noses of the Lancastrian main force.

to Barkston Ash, another piece of high ground is exposed in a similar fashion to that at Barkston Ash that we mentioned earlier. I believe that there is a link to these views and Clifford's demise. There has always been a lot of speculation regarding the death of Lords Clifford and Neville. Not only has the location of their demise been debated, but also the question, why were they not supported by the main Lancastrian force as they retreated? If we remember the contemporary reference to his death as shown in the previous chapter:

> '...Lord Clifford, either from heat or pain, put off his gorget, was suddenly hit by an arrow, as some say, without a head...'

It has always intrigued me as to why Clifford would take time to remove his gorget whilst engaged in a running skirmish. In answering this I put forward the following suggestion. It is evident that the Lancastrians who defended the bridge had learned that the Yorkists had crossed the river upstream at Castleford, and consequently began to withdraw. As this force retreated back towards the main Lancastrian line, I have concluded that they were unaware of the fact that Fauconberg was in close and determined pursuit, and had in fact got ahead of them.

I asked the reader to consider the view of the terrain as we drove into Barkston Ash, and again the view mentioned above. Could it be that the retreating Lancastrians stopped for a short rest at either of these locations. Further, that the Yorkists – in pursuit – came over the brow of either hill and caught them off guard leading to the deaths of the two lords? This scenario would certainly explain why Clifford had removed his gorget, (as he rested) and would, in my opinion, explain why they were wiped out to a man. They were simply ambushed.

I don't think it will be ever proved categorically where this ambush took place but the geographical similarities with regard to a sharp incline at both locations, does, in my opinion, add weight to the theory. If you look to the north, (behind you), it is clear that there is another (albeit more gentle) slope up towards where the Lancastrian main force would have been encamped. Clearly, even if the ambush took place at Scarthingwell on or around the location where you are currently standing, this location (and the one at Barkston Ash) are out of sight of the main Lancastrian force and, in my opinion, explains why they didn't come to their assistance, they were simply unaware of what had transpired until after the event. Boardman in his work, *The Battle of Towton*, writes with regard to the ambush site of Clifford and Neville:

> 'Another place cited as Lord Clifford's demise is Dintingdale, the land between Scarthingwell and Barkston Ash, in particular the area marked by a derelict stone cross foundation plinth, commonly called 'The Leper Pot'. This curiosity may once have supported an upright cross situated in the still visible hollowed-out block of limestone, and may in fact have been erected to commemorate Clifford's death there in 1461.

Unfortunately, neither local tradition nor chronicles support the theory.

That the Leper Pot was a base for a cross at some time, locating the position of Clifford's death exactly, rather than Dintingdale, which is such a large area of land, is an interesting concept. We must, however, temper this idea with stories of a possible grave pit containing the bodies of Lord Clifford, John Neville and others of their contingent near present-day Dintingdale itself. In 1835 an amateur excavation

'Butcher' Clifford's force was returning down this road to join up with the Lancastrian army just over the hill at Towton. Either at this location, or earlier at the 'Leper Pot'(or along the whole stretch of road between the two), Lord Fauconberg's mounted archers, who had made good time up the old Roman road, got ahead and ambushed 'The Flower of Craven' wiping them within a mile of safety. The deaths of Richard of York and his son Edmund at the hands of Clifford, at the battle of Wakefield, was thus avenged.

was carried out in the vicinity and a pit was dug close to the turnpike road. In it were found bones supposed to have been the remains of Lord Clifford, perhaps identified because of the absence of the skull (taken to decorate Micklegate Bar, York). Here, though, we have evidence of the existence of a burial pit of some kind, with remains of some sort, near the battle zone, thus contradictions regarding the Clifford Cross theory can be brought to bear, especially as Clifford family tradition states that, 'The Butcher was tumbled into a pit of promiscuous dead bodies after the battle of Towton'. It is doubtful that men carried these bodies very far from their place of death after the skirmish at Dintingdale. [8]

However, having now fully considered Clifford's and Neville's fate, **return to your car** and travel along the road **towards Saxton**. The road you are travelling along is called Saxton Lane. The area between Saxton and Scarthingwell along which you are travelling is Dintingdale. Continue along the road and it will bring you to a staggered cross-roads in the middle of the village. Opposite you, and to the left, is the Church of All Saints, where Lord Dacre's tomb lies, along with a large grave pit.

We should leave this for a while and travel across the staggered junction past the church down Dam Street, (formally Silver Street) out of the village along the country road until you come to a T junction. Turn left, and travel away from Towton on the B1217, until you pass the large lay-by on your right and reach the Crooked Billet public house. Pull into the car park here, as opposite this public house is the remains of the village of Lead – if you have taken the route that Lord Fauconberg's vanguard may have taken – as is next to be described – then to this is where you will be directed.

Alternative route from the River Aire. The advance of Lord Fauconberg via Castleford

The alternative route to Towton takes us through Castleford. From the bridge, rather than go forwards towards the A1, **turn right** and retrace your steps along the **B6136**, until you come to the roundabout where you would have turned left to travel back to the motorway. Instead, carry **straight on towards Castleford** (along the **A639**) until you reach another roundabout just past the Royal Oak public house (which is on your left) and **turn right** following the **A656** towards **Castleford** town centre. You are actually on Pontefract Road but travelling away from Pontefract. Continue along this road past the Church of St. Paul the Apostle, (which appears on your right) until you reach a roundabout. At the roundabout **turn left** (again as if heading towards the town centre). At the **next roundabout**, you will continue **straight ahead** but now following the signs for The North, A1 and York. As you cross the bridge, approximately where the ford would have been, you are travelling over the River Aire – out of Castleford – across a second bridge under which the canal runs. Continue along this road **past Allerton Bywater** and through two light controlled cross-roads (**still on the A656**).

Travel for several miles along a straight road, which follows very closely the path of the old Roman road, and this accounts for the very straight nature of it, past Ledston Luck village, (and the old colliery, now a small industrial park) and **straight across** at the next roundabout. Continue along the **A656**, past the Peckfield Business Park, and you will notice that you will soon be travelling along a recently constructed road which leads you to a large roundabout under which flows the new **A1/M1** link motorway. This is **junction 47** of that motorway, and at this roundabout you should **turn right** onto the **B1217**, following the signs for Towton, Aberford and Lotherton Hall. As you pass Lotherton Hall (on your right) you are approximately 2½ miles from the Crooked Billet, and when you arrive at the Crooked Billet, **pull into the car park**, so that you can continue the tour and explore the remains of Lead village – a significant campsite for the Yorkist army before the battle of Towton.

The Crooked Billet and Lead village

Having parked at either the public house, or in the lay-by further up the road, you are conveniently located to explore the surrounding areas. In the field opposite the entrance to the Crooked Billet public house you will note the isolated and lowly church of St. Mary's.

This is all that remains of the village of Lead. To get to the church you must first cross the River Cock (now Cock Beck) via the bridge at this point. The Cock Beck marks the western boundary of the battlefield – a subject we will cover in detail later. You can then walk across the field and explore both the inside and the outside of the church. Inside the church are a number of decorative plaques commemorating a number of the nobles who fought at the battle of Towton.

On the night of 28-29 March 1461, the surrounding areas extending all the way to Saxton and beyond would have been covered with Yorkist bivouacs as they tried as best they could to rest and prepare themselves for the battle that would follow. It has been suggested that the village would have been temporarily deserted by its inhabitants some short time before the Yorkists arrived and if that was the case, then it is very likely that the dwellings would have been used by the Yorkist soldiers to provide shelter on that cold night. The village itself was finally abandoned, fell into disrepair and disappeared sometime in the 16th Century. However, John Leland in his work *Itinerary*, noted around that time that some dwellings existed and were occupied:

> 'Lead, a hamlet, where Skargill had a fair manor place of timber. Cock Beck after crookith by Saxton and Towton village fields, and goith into Wharfe river a mile

Yorkist positions

The Yorkist positions as seen from Lead Church. On the night of 28th/29th March 1461 these fields surrounding the church would have been filled with camp fires and soldiers huddled up against the freezing cold night.

Interior and exterior views of St Mary's Church, Lead. No doubt some of the Yorkist leaders spent the night prior to the battle in this building resting and praying for victory.

beneath Tadcaster.'

Although Lead features in the Towton campaign as only a billet for the soldiers the night before the battle, it is said that the site is an ancient battlefield in its own right. During the wars of Stephen and Matilda in the twelfth century, there was an engagement fought on or around this location between those two sides.

Having visited the church we can return to the Crooked Billet public house. Local tradition states that an inn on this site was the location of the Earl of Warwick's billet the night before the battle and that the word 'Crooked' is actually a reference to the Ragged Staff emblem used by the Warwick household troops and soldiers as their banner, and 'billet', an obvious reference to the fact that he stayed there. However, there is no contemporary evidence to suggest that there was an inn at Lead at the time of the battle, or indeed, any inn located on what is now the B1217 road upon which the modern-day Crooked Billet public house now stands.

The words 'crooked billet' however, do have another meaning, and in the old Yorkshire dialogue the words 'Crooked Billet' are actually spelt 'Greukt Billets' meaning crossed sticks. This is interesting, in so much as the Warwick contingent also had a white cross (or crossed sticks) on a red background as one of their emblems. It would appear that there is a connection between the inn and the Warwick contingent, but without contemporary evidence to provide the link, then the connection can only be speculative. However, putting this aside, the Crooked Billet public house is well worth a visit either before or after exploring the battlefield, and as such we will leave the reader here while we progress our understanding of the events that took place at the actual battle of Towton.

See Chapter Six, page 77

EXPLORING THE BATTLEFIELD OF TOWTON

From the car park of the Crooked Billet, follow the B1217 towards Towton. As you approach Castle Hill Farm (on your left) the ground will begin to rise. You are now travelling up the south slope of the raised land north of Saxton, on top of

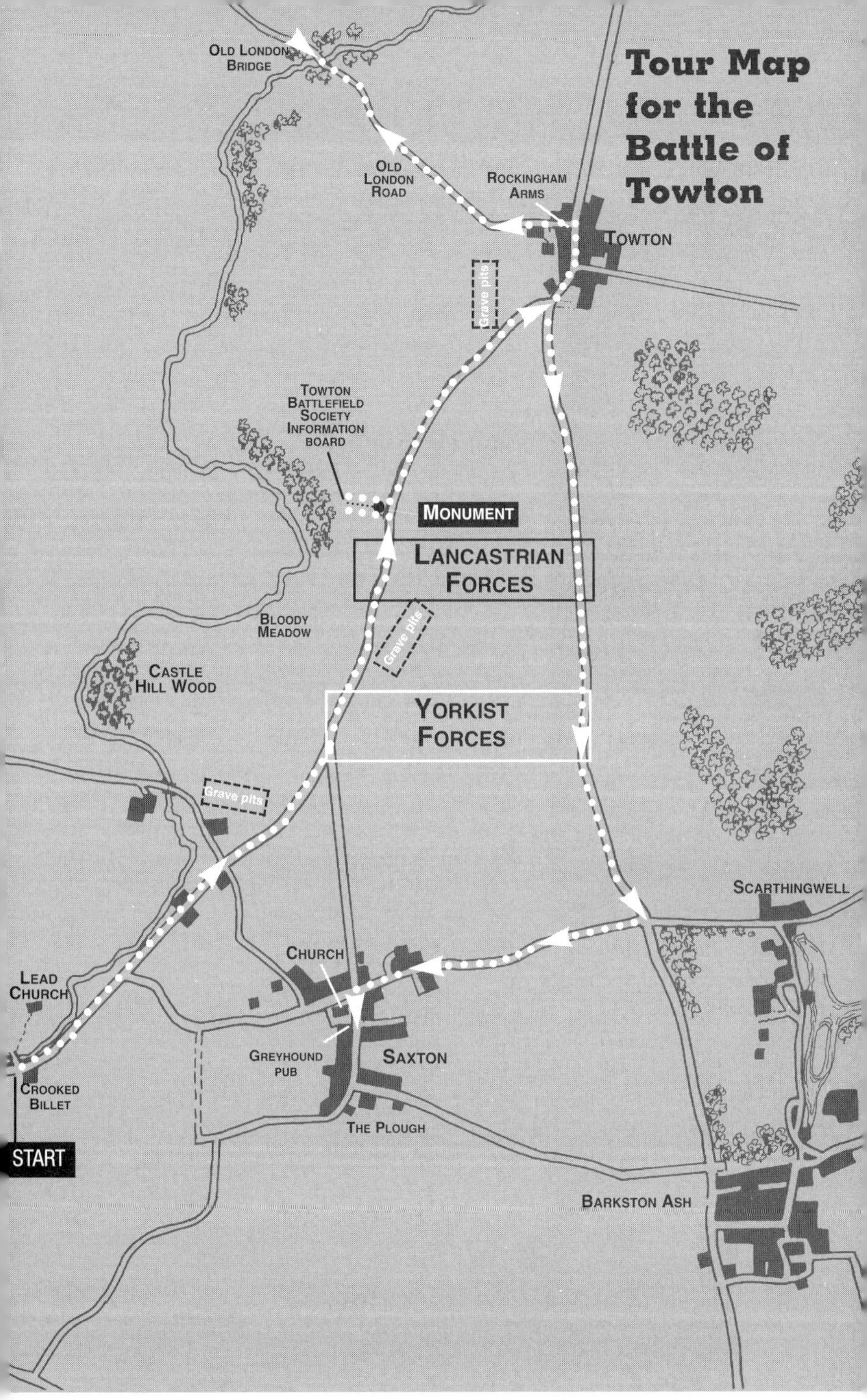

Tour Map for the Battle of Towton
Old London Bridge
Old London Road
Rockingham Arms
Towton
Grave pits
Towton Battlefield Society Information Board
Monument
Lancastrian Forces
Grave pits
Bloody Meadow
Castle Hill Wood
Yorkist Forces
Grave pits
Scarthingwell
Church
Lead Church
Greyhound pub
Saxton
Crooked Billet
Start
The Plough
Barkston Ash

Memorial cross commemorating the battle of Towton, the origin of which remains a mystery.

which the Yorkist army assembled at the start of the battle. This location is approximately one mile from the Crooked Billet. To your left you will see Castle Hill Wood and the slope down towards the Cock Beck. Between. the area of ground immediately before the slope, and where you are now travelling, is Bloody Meadow.

The Monument

Continue **along the B1217** for about half a mile towards the monument located on your left. As you travel along the B1217 towards the monument, you will notice that the ground dips then rises again. The high ground to the north that you are approaching is the high ground upon which the Lancastrian forces assembled before the battle. As previously mentioned, on your left there will shortly come into view a monument, this is known locally as 'Lord Dacre's Cross', and you should **park your car** at the side of the road at this point. This monument is relatively modern, but the head of the monument is a stone cross dating back to the mediaeval period. It was found nearby in a ditch and the cross itself was

Bloody Meadow

erected by a New Zealander who visited the site in the 1960s.

The wording on the base of the monument (located on its south face) has become much eroded in recent years, and I fear that it will not be long before it is unreadable. It states: 'Battle of Towton Palm Sunday 1461'. As you stand by the monument, facing the Yorkist positions, you are actually located to the rear right flank of the Lancastrian lines, and the location of the monument should not fool the reader into thinking that you are in the centre of the battlefield.

Bloody Meadow

As you stand by the monument facing the Yorkist positions, to your right (westwards) you will notice a **dirt road** leading off towards the direction of the Cock Beck. You should follow this track to the point where it ends – overlooking the Cock Beck itself. At this location, the **Towton Battlefield Society** has erected a board showing a detailed map of the area and the location of the various forces in relation to it. This board is excellent for those unfamiliar with the battlefield for orientation purposes (see page 152).

Immediately to your front you get an excellent view of Bloody Meadow, and the steep incline that descends down to the Cock Beck. Try to imagine the slaughter at this point and the desperate struggle of the Lancastrian soldiers as they fought for their lives in this area as their line collapsed. You

When the Lancastrian ranks finally broke men fled the field of carnage down into this valley meadow. Yorkist troops, in hot pursuit, caught many of them down by the Cock Beck, which was a raging torrent at the time of the battle, and a great slaughter took place.

can tell from the incline just how desperate their position had become, and we can only imagine the scenes of slaughter that took place here during the battle and the rout as many solders from both sides would no doubt have tumbled down this incline towards the Cock Beck – the Lancastrians in hope of escape and the jubilant Yorkists in hope of plunder. Do not be fooled by the somewhat sedate view of the Cock Beck that you get from here. At the time of the battle we are told that it was in flood and would have been significantly wider and deeper than what you see today. Clearly, as a scene of a great deal of carnage one would expect grave pits to be present in the Bloody Meadow area, and indeed this is the case, and there is evidence in the lie of the ground of several grave pits in this area – maybe as many as five. Today, they are difficult to locate, however, they did not go unnoticed by John Leland, who wrote the following in regard to them when he visited the battlefield in Tudor times and wrote:

> 'They lay afore in 5 pits, yet appearing half a mile by north in Saxton Field...' [10]

Castle Hill Wood

Again, looking towards the Yorkist positions you will have a clear view (to the right) of Castle Hill Wood. The current wood is much reduced from the one that was here at the time of the battle, and it is from this wood that the Lancastrians are said to have launched a surprise flanking attack on the Yorkists left flank. It has always been a wonder to me how the Lancastrians could have kept a force, unnoticed, in this wood prior to the attack. Even if we bear in mind the semi-evergreen nature of the foliage, I still find it difficult to understand how the Yorkists never spotted them.

There are a number of theories with regard to this, but the one that I favour is, that if the attack took place at all, then the Lancastrian force did not start the battle at that place, but travelled to it during the course of the mêlée. If you remember that you are standing at the rear right flank of the Lancastrian position, at the start of the battle the valley below you to your right, would have been out of sight of the Yorkists' forces. Is it more probable that the Lancastrians concealed their ambush party down in the valley, and during the course of the battle they travelled along the valley floor to a point at the back of Castle Hill Wood, scaled the hill and came charging through the woods to engage the Yorkist on their left flank

In recent years there has been discovered the remains of a bridge at that point, indicating that perhaps there was a footpath at the rear of the hill upon which Castle Hill Wood is located. I don't think there is any other way the Lancastrians could have carried out this surprise attack other than the one described. Again, this will probably become a debating point for many years to come. During the battle of Tewkesbury in 1470, Edward was once again facing a Lancastrian force. Again, on his left flank was a wood. At this battle however, he sent two hundred spearmen to secure the wood on the Yorkists behalf. Maybe he had learnt a hard lesson at the battle of Towton after all.

Chapel Hill and Towton Hall

As you **return to your car look** to the left (north) and you can clearly see Towton Hall and the raised ground immediately to the left of it is another site of interest inthe battle. This raised point is Chapel Hill. Chapel Hill and its surrounding areas are the location of the resting places of thousands of those who died in the battle. We should not be surprised at this, as those who fled the field would have come this way and as we know, many more died in the rout than the battle itself, therefore we can conclude that this area was littered with bodies by the time the battle had concluded.

During the reign of Richard III, the king instructed that a chapel should be raised on this spot to commemorate both his brother's famous victory, and the fact that so many of those who had died were buried at this place – hence the name Chapel Hill. Unfortunately, by the time of his death at the battle of Bosworth in 1485, the chapel had not been completed, and no doubt there were no more funds forthcoming for its completion under the regime of Henry Tudor. Due to this fact, the building works were abandoned and the chapel fell in to disrepair and eventually all visible evidence of its existence vanished as the stone would have been used to complete other buildings in the surrounding areas. It is suggested that the cross placed at the top of the monument was in fact a decorative cross from this chapel. This seems to me to be a logical assumption, however, other views suggest that it was originally from a monument erected to commemorate the death of Lord Clifford that was originally either located in Dintingdale or Barkston Ash. Another debating point for modern historians.

There is absolutely no doubt that Chapel Hill and Towton Hall are the location of large amounts of skeletons, Brooke on his visits to the battlefield and this area wrote:

> 'Near the village of Towton, and on its south-west side, King Richard III commenced building a chapel, in memory of the slain who had fallen in the battle, but it was never finished and the place where it was commenced is now called the 'Chapel Garth' or 'Chapel Hill'.
>
> 'It is situated close to, and extends in the rear or westward of, Towton Hall, which stands on part of the site of it; and a considerable mass of human bones was found, about sixty years ago, in enlarging the cellars of Towton Hall. Behind the Garden, and on the west side, are some inequalities in the ground, seemingly denoting the site of a small building; and in digging there, tiles and worked stones have been discovered: strongly conveying the impression, that the walls and

foundations of the chapel had been placed there.' [11]

In discussing various excavations of graves on the battlefield, he goes on to say:

'...that about a year or two before (Drake wrote his work *Eboracum* in 1736), he (Drake) and two other gentlemen had the curiosity to go and see a fresh grave opened, in those fields, where amongst vast quantities of bones, they found some arrow piles, pieces of broken swords, and five very fresh groat pieces of Henry IV., V., and VI's coin. These were laid near together, close to the thighbone, which made them conjecture, that there had not been time to strip the dead, before they were tossed into the pit... (This is contra to everything that we have been told about the graves on Towton field. Although some artefacts have been found, we are led to believe that because the burials of the slain took longer than usual, due to the fact that there were so many dead to be buried and that the ground was very hard due to the fact that it was in the winter months, there was therefore, plenty of time to strip and search all the bodies. Armour and weapons were very much sought after and would have been taken off the bodies of the slain as would any items of value, coins rings etc – this explains why even today, very little in the way of artefacts is to be found on the battlefield)...It is to be regretted, that he has not informed us, in what particular spot, those relics were dug up; but as he, in the preceding sentence, had mentioned the intended chapel, and the piece of ground called 'Chapel Garth', it is only reasonable to conclude, that he alluded to the latter.' [12]

Indeed, the same site (Towton Hall), was the scene of a great

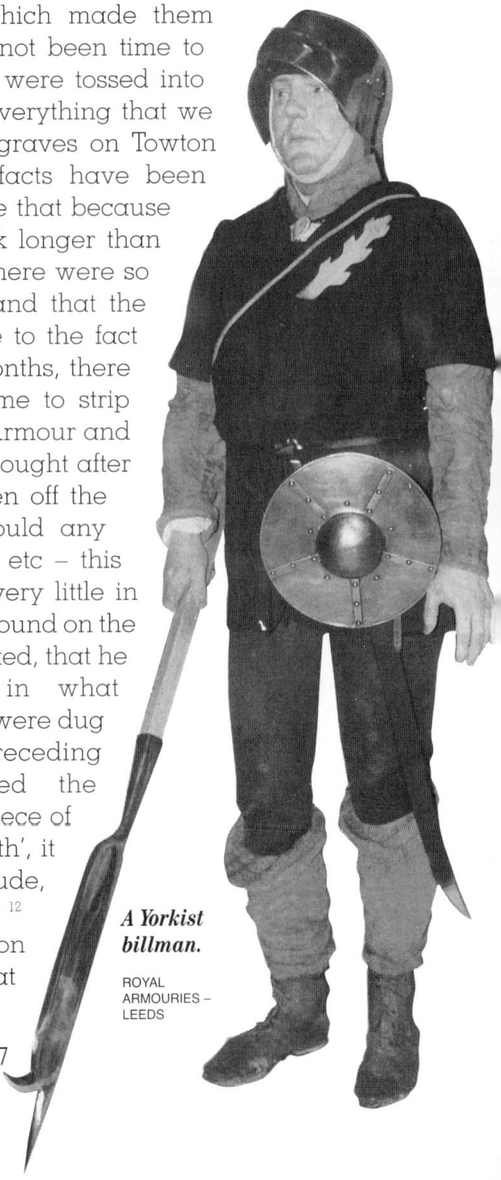

A Yorkist billman.

ROYAL ARMOURIES – LEEDS

deal of archaeological activity in more modern times, when in July of 1996, a previously unrecorded mass grave containing approximately twenty-three bodies was uncovered during the building of an extension to the north-east side of Towton Hall. The construction company obtained a Home Office licence for the removal of the bodies, and they were subsequently exhumed and reburied next to Lord Dacre's tomb in Saxton Church. However, further work by the construction company identified further bodies, and, at that point, North Yorkshire County Council Heritage Unit was contacted, and they attended the site early in July 1996 – and permission was given by the developer for a proper archaeological excavation of the site within the development area. There are several grave pits in this location, but permission to carry out a study was only given on the one grave that had been unearthed by the construction company.

The grave that was thus uncovered appears to have occupied a space of some 3.25 metres by 2.0 metres and was lying in a north-west to south-east orientation and truncated to the west – and the bodies were found at a depth of 0.65 metres below modern ground level, and the grave contained some forty-three bodies – along with thirteen potsherds, seven fragments of animal bone, six ferrous objects, eleven copper alloy objects. The majority of the bodies lay in an east/west direction, with their heads facing to the west, and after the individual details of each body was recorded, the bodies were removed to the Calvin Wells Laboratory at the University of Bradford for further analysis.

The initial analysis concluded that the individuals removed from the grave pit were between eighteen and forty-three years of age and had died of either:

1. Blunt force trauma caused by weapons such as a mace or a ball hammer.

2. Wounds by sharp-edged weapons such as daggers and swords.

3. Penetrating injuries such as arrows or a pole axe.

Many of the bodies had multiple injuries, (but very few to the lower half of the body) and many of the skulls had suffered repeated blows – each potentially fatal. More interestingly, was the fact that many of the bodies had previous wounds that had healed, leading us to conclude that these soldiers had seen previous military action before their fatal encounters at Towton. Of the other artefacts that were recovered a number were arrowheads, (one of which was found embedded in the spine of one of the bodies) and one single copper ring. This absence of 'artefacts' supports the fact that the bodies were stripped of anything useful, cloths, weapons, armour etc before burial.

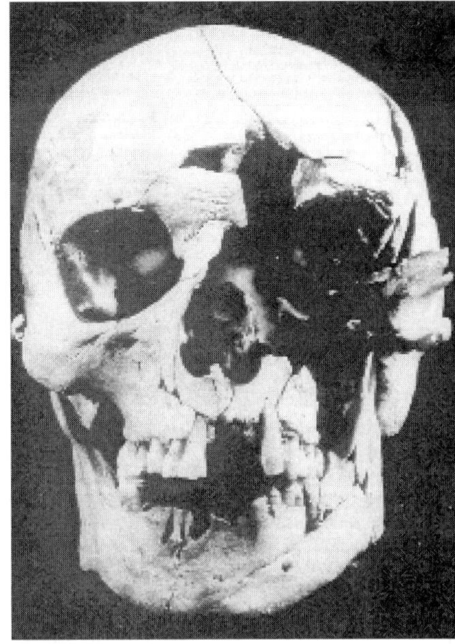

Towton skull bearing evidence of earlier wounds that had healed, indicating that he was a professional soldier. Detailed work was carried out on this and other remains by the University of Bradford.

Equally, the discovery of the grave and its contents has presented a whole new set of debating points – chief amongst these are:

1. Are these bodies of Lancastrians or Yorkists?

The grave is located over a mile from the 'battlefield', so we can conclude that these bodies are those of soldiers who died in the rout, which does not necessarily mean that they are all Lancastrians. However, that fact alone would suggest that the majority of them are.

2. Why are there so many injuries on these individuals? (one of the bodies had ten head wounds alone).

Many of the injuries were to the head, therefore leading us to conclude that these individuals had no head protection to start with, or that it was removed. It is not difficult to imagine several men in pursuit of, and falling on, a single victim, removing his helmet and then carrying out a savage attack which resulted in his death.

3. Bearing in mind the aforementioned question about lack of head protection – is it possible that these individuals were indeed captured, and then subsequently massacred?

The fact that there were very few injuries to the lower parts of the bodies added to the fact that there is evidence of defence wounds to the upper arms, (as if they had tried to protect themselves in the absence of weapons) has led to the suggestion that these poor souls were indeed captured, stripped of their arms, swords etc, then put to death.

However, by looking at all the evidence, the fact that on many of the bodies there is an absence of wounds to the chest and back areas, leads me to conclude that protection to the upper parts of the bodies, by armour, jacks and brigandines etc, (which we know the soldiers at the battle of Towton wore) was in place. Which leads me to further conclude, that no massacre took place – as surely these would have been removed also, prior to these individuals being slain.

In any event, it is not to be doubted that this was a major archaeological discovery which has added greatly to our understanding of how the soldiers at the battle of Towton died. However, it will not be until a similar excavation on a grave on the actual battlefield itself is carried out that we know the whole truth.

The Bridge of Bodies

Chapel Hill and Towton Hall are private property, and as such, they cannot be examined up close. Therefore, we should at this point, **return to our car** and continue along the **B1217** (later the A162) into Towton village itself, and pull into the car park of the **Rockingham Arms** public house – which is located on the left hand side of the road as you enter the village, just short of a mile from the monument. To the rear of the car park is a **small road** (which later becomes a footpath, signposted Public Bridleway – Stutton) that follows the path of the Old London Road, and we should **take this path** down to the Cock Beck and the scene of yet more slaughter. After a **walk of about a ½ mile**, during which the footpath begins to descend steeply towards the Cock Beck, you will enter a wood and ultimately come across the bridge over the beck at this point. We should recall that Richard Brooke wrote the following regarding this:

> 'The descent by the ancient road is so steep, that it is a matter of surprise, how the heavy coaches formally in use, and wagons, could safely pass up and down it, yet

it was even in modern times part of the great north road. After descending the eminence, the ancient road formerly crossed the River Cock by a stone bridge, now destroyed, and after passing over a beautiful meadow ground before noticed, it ascended the rising ground on the opposite side of the meadow, and so proceeded on towards Tadcaster.

'At present the River Cock is crossed in the meadow by a narrow wooden bridge, merely used for foot passengers and horses, the supporting piers of which are of stone, and they probably were built or rebuilt from the materials of the older bridge; in fact I saw several worked and broken stones lying near it, strengthening the supposition of their having formed part of an old bridge...'

Brooke goes on to say:

'The steep descent from the village by the old road, must have been very perilous, under such circumstances; their cavalry, many of the horses doubtless wounded and ungovernable, and their infantry, all attempting to descend by a steep road, hotly

The present-day wooden bridge over the Cock Beck. Tranquil now but once the scene of horrific events as the defeated Lancastrians strove to cross with the victorious Yorkists in pursuit. See the illustration on page 90.

pushed by enemies, who gave no quarter would be lost, and a scene of confusion and carnage would naturally result.

The strong probability is that there was not then a bridge over the Cock; but if there was one, we must conclude that it was of small size, and that it could not have been wide enough to allow so numerous a crowd to pass; and if there were not one and all of them were obliged to attempt to ford the stream, the danger would of course be increased... [Brooke then quotes the work of an earlier historian called Biondi]: "...Those who remained alive took the road for the bridge of Tadcaster, but being unable to reach it, and believing a small river called Cock to be fordable, the greater part were drowned therein.

It is constantly affirmed, that those who survived, passed over by treading on the dead bodies of the sufferer; the water of this stream, and of the River Wharfe, into which it empties itself, were coloured in a manner to appear as pure blood."' [13]

As we stand on the modern day crossing of the stretch of water at this point, you will be fooled, as I have, by the gentle flow of the water, into believing that this is a tranquil place. We can only imagine the scene that would have presented itself on and around this point around 550 years ago on that cold Palm Sunday afternoon.

North Acres and Lord Dacre's Tree

Return to your car and a welcome break at the Rockingham Arms. **Turn right out** of the car park back along the way that we came. However, rather than turning left back onto the B1217, you should **continue** along, southwards on the **A162**. As you pass **Saxton Grange**, on your left, approximately a mile from the Rockingham Arms, you are travelling through the middle of the Lancastrian left hand ranks as they were positioned at the start of the battle.

From this point, then stretching over the hill to the monument, (which is out of sight beyond the rise in the land) was the full length of the Lancastrian line. Along this line but closer to the B1217 are located yet more grave pits. On the map of the area drawn by Thomas Jefferies, made during the

1730s, these are shown as 'The Graves in Towton Field'. According to the Harlain Manuscript (MS 795):

> 'Certain deep trenches overgrown with bushes and briers containing 19 yards in breadth and 32 yards in length in Towton Field, a bow shot on the left hand in the way betwixt Saxton and Towton, half mile short of Towton...'

This solitary tree is believed to be the descendent of the one used by a boy, armed with a crossbow, as a vantage point to snipe and kill Lord Dacre. GW

Continue along the A162 and shortly after Saxton Grange, you will see on your right hand side the low point between the two raised areas upon which the two armies started the battle.

This is North Acres and the scene of much conflict during the battle. North Acres leads into Towton Dale and then on into Bloody Meadow. As we drive past here, we should recall that North Acres was also the location on the battlefield where Lord Dacre was shot and killed. The ancestor of the burr tree, that was the vantage point of the sniper who shot him, remains to be seen at this location.

Saxton Church

Continue along the A162, until you come to **Scarthingwell cross-roads**. At this point we should **turn right** and travel through Dintingdale along Saxton Lane into the village of Saxton itself. However, before we do this, we should consider that it would have been approximately across this junction, towards the centre of the battlefield, that Sir John Howard would have led the Duke of Norfolk's contingent to join in the mêlée – which eventually caused the break up of the Lancastrian front line.

Continue along Saxton Lane, and consider the high

Saxton Church. The area in the foreground was used to bury casualties from the Battle of Towton.

ground to your right. It was on that rise where the Yorkists assembled their army at the very start of the battle, and on which they were pushed back before the arrival of Norfolk's contingent – which saved the day for the Yorkist cause.

On entering the village, you should **park your car** in a manner that makes it convenient to explore the church of All Saints. Featuring prominently in the north east corner of the graveyard is the tomb of Lord Dacre. Sadly, the tomb is in a poor state of repair. Some years ago I discovered a photographic record of it taken in 1918 by the Heckmondwike Photographic Society. In their photographs of the tomb, the detail can be seen clearly. It is a marvel, and a concern, that in the year 1918, the tomb, having stood for 457 years, could still be seen in all it's glory and it's detail was still legible, and that in the last eighty-three years the pollutants in the air have weathered it away so that almost nothing now remains to be viewed on the exterior of the tomb. It is at times like this that we require the works of Brooke to refer to, for he wrote in regards to the tomb:

> 'The tomb of Lord Dacre, called by Stow a "meane tombe" (meaning not a contemptible, or shabby tomb, for it certainly has been a handsome one, but one of medium size), also lies on the north side of the church,

and is very near the place where the slain were buried. It is about two feet high, with the inscription a good deal worn, so that I was not able to read many words, [this is difficult to understand considering the photographic record of 1918, and perhaps it indicates that he could not understand the coarse latin rather than see the inscription itself], it stands with it sides nearly corresponding with the four points of the compass; it has armorial bearings on each of its sides; and, besides various other quartering, which are much defaced by age and weather, I observed the quarters-1st and 4th, Chequy, or and gules, for vaux of Gilsland; 2nd and 3rd, Gules, three escallops argent, for Dacre, which though not very plain, are nevertheless still visible; and I consider the engravings of the tomb in Dr. Whitaker's work, very like the original. The tomb is of dark stone or marble, and the slab or lid is very heavy, but broken in two pieces, at about two-thirds its length; and it seems likely to sustain further injury from boys playing and climbing upon it. It is much to be regretted, that some endeavour is not made by some person of taste, to preserve it by putting iron rails round it [which has since been done] some of the leaders [naturally supposed to be Yorkists] were interred in the church; and within the recollection of Mr. Kendall [the owner of Towton Hall] some slabs, with inscriptions in the Old English letters, were in existence there, which are said to have covered their remains.' [14]

The tower of Saxton Church appears to have been rebuilt after the Reformation, and, as is said, between two hundred and fifty and three hundred years ago. Several representations of crosses have been cut upon slabs or stones which are built into the tower, and which were evidently carved in memory of some of the slain, who were buried there; most probably Yorkist knights or leaders.

Lancastrian Sir John Neville, commonly called John, Lord Neville, is said not to have been buried there, but at the chapel of Lead, which is about half a mile from Saxton. This I believe, is a reference to the work of John Leland, who stated in his work *Itinerary*, that it was the belief of those he interviewed in the village that John, Lord Neville was buried in the grounds of Lead Church also. However, some hold to the opinion that John Lord Clifford, Neville's friend and 'partner in crime', slain with him at Dintingdale, is buried in the church yard at All Saints, Saxton. Yet another debating point regarding the battle and battlefield.

Dr. Whitaker...gives the following as the correct inscription (on Dacre's tomb)

> HIC JACET RANULPHUS DOMINUS DE DACRE ET GREYSTOCKE VERUS MILES QUI OBIIT IN BELLO PRO REGE SUO HENRICO SEXTO ANNO MCCCCLXI VICESIMO DIE MENSIS MARCH VID'LT., DOMINICA PALMARUM CUJUS ANIME PROPICIETUR DEUS. AMEN

From the mention of Henry VI, it can be surmised that the tomb was not erected until after the death of Edward IV. I am somewhat surprised that Brooke says this, as I do not believe that the Yorkists would mind either way about the burial of any Lancastrian noble.

Drake mentions that many years ago, this tomb was violently wrenched open (for it had been strongly clamped together with iron) in order to inter beneath it a Mr. Gascoyne, when the remains of Dacre's body was found, in a standing posture, and that a fragment of the slab, and a material part of the inscription, were then broken off.

He does not inform us who or what Mr. Gascoyne was, when alive, but whoever he was, whether high or low sphere in life, whether he was a gentleman or a rag merchant, it evinced bad taste on the part of his relations or representatives, to commit such an act; and perhaps some culpable remissness on the part of the then incumbent of the church to permit it.

A translation of the inscription reads: 'Here lies Randolf, Lord of Dacre and Gilsland, a true knight, valiant in battle in the service of King Henry VI, who died on Palm Sunday, 29th March 1461, on whose soul may God have mercy, Amen'. [15]

Brooke mentions the discovery of the body of Dacre standing in an upright position. In 1861 there was discovered – adjacent to the tomb – the remains of a horse, the skull of which now resides in the British Museum. Local tradition does claim that Dacre was buried astride his horse, though it appears that this is not the case even though the two do appear to share the same ground. The fact that Dacre is buried here does add credence to the fact that he fell during the battle and not after it, as it does appear that there was time to remove his body from the battlefield and care for it – and it was not 'tossed' into one of the larger grave pits on the field itself.

We should not be surprised as to the fact that care was given to the burial of such Lancastrian nobles such as Dacre. After all, once the Yorkists had moved on from the battlefield, the area, like much of Yorkshire, remained very much pro-Lancastrian in its sympathies. In the southeast corner of the graveyard you will notice that there are no modern gravestones, this is because this is one large grave pit. In describing it, John Leland wrote:

> 'In the churchyard were many of the bones of men killed at Palmsunday Field buried.' [16]

There has to my knowledge, been only one excavation to seek the extent of the grave pit located in the church yard,

Lord Dacre's grave. Human remains found when a grave pit was discovered at Towton Hall are also interred at this spot.

which is not to be wondered at, bearing in mind that we are on consecrated ground. Again Brooke wrote of this excavation:

> 'Their bones were exposed to view, lying about four feet below the surface, in making a vault not many years ago, and again subsequently, in making another in 1848...
>
> ...we may conclude that they were Yorkists of some consideration, from the circumstance of the survivors taking the trouble of interring the remains in consecrated ground, at some little distance from the field of battle. The persons whose bones were so exposed, must have been either young, or in the prime of life, because the skulls were remarkable for the soundness and excellence of the teeth.' [17]

You will notice that the ground to the right of Dacre's tomb has recently been disturbed. This is because this is the site of reburial of the twenty-three soldiers excavated from the grave pit at Towton Hall that we discussed earlier. Many visitors to Towton, wonder as to what treasures are held in such grave pits, and what remnants of the battle lie deep beneath the ground. Over the years a number of artefacts have been found, but due to the fact that the bodies were generally stripped before burial, very little when compared to the numbers who fought at the battle site. On this subject Brooke commented that:

> 'Instances have occurred, though not very numerous of late, of the discovery of parts of human skeletons and fragments of armour, weapons, piles of arrows, bridle bits, spurs etc, etc, on the field of battle.'

The remains of armour, weapons and relics, turned up on the field of this great engagement, have been rather small, which has been very fairly accounted for by Dr. Whitaker who wrote an account of the battle previous to Brooke's visit to the battlefield. From the fact that the weather had been cold and the victory so complete, hunting for and taking spoil from the field bu the victors, along with the internment of the dead, would have proceeded at a more leisurely pace than usual. He does however mentions one relic, which escaped the vigilance of the plunderers, viz., a gold ring, weighing about one ounce, which was found on the field about thirty years

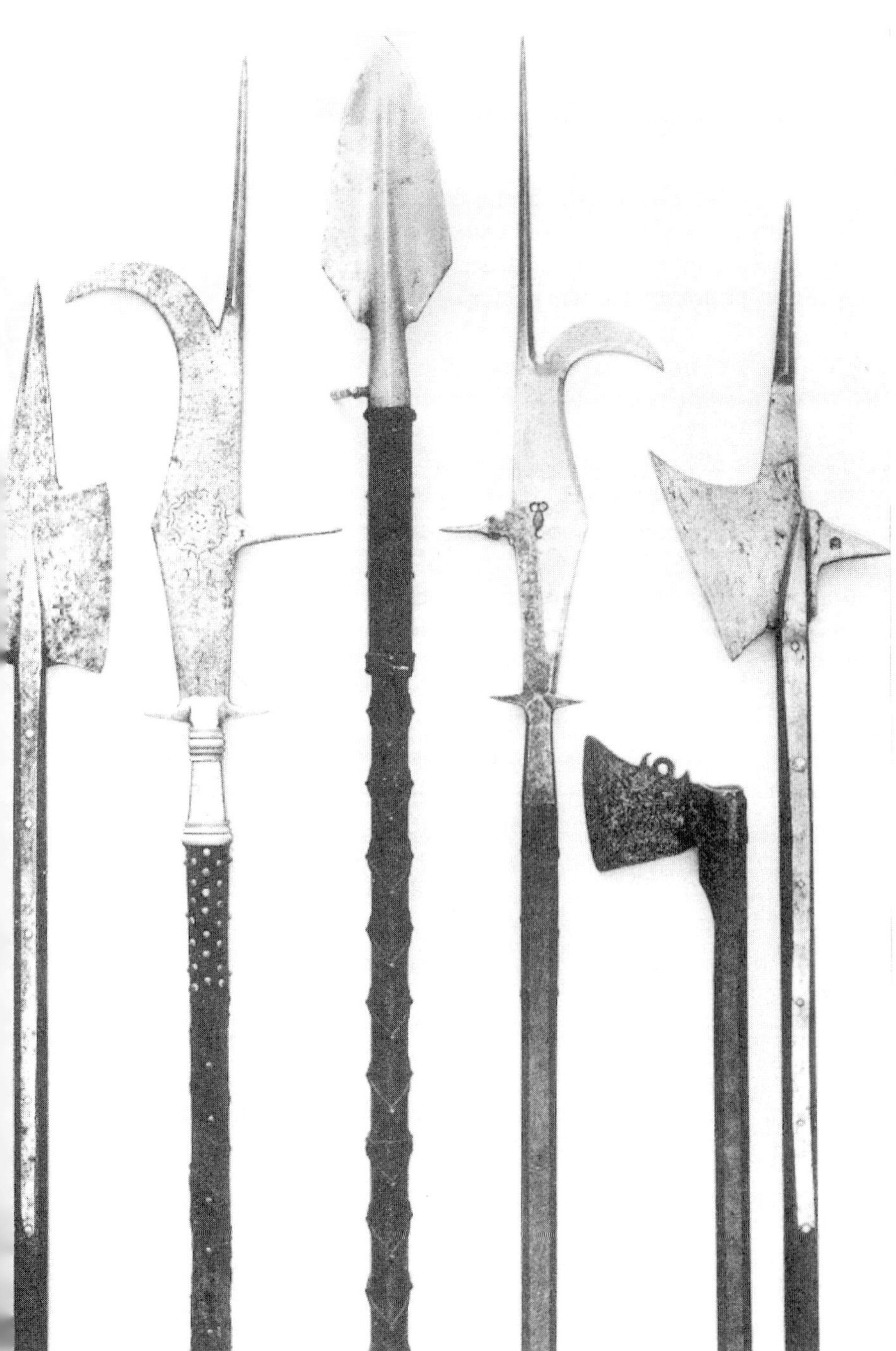

Type of weapons used during the wars of the Roses period.

before his work was published in 1816. It had no stone, but a lion passant was cut upon the gold, with this inscription in the old black letter character, 'Now ys thus'. The crest is that of the Percies; and Dr Whitaker considers, that it was the ring actually worn by the Earl of Northumberland; and that the motto seems to allude to the times, as if it were expressed, 'This age is fierce as a lion'...

'A dagger or short sword, discovered on the field is now in the possession of the Rev. W J Newman, of Badsworth, Yorkshire, it is 2 feet 4 and a half inches long, including the portion which was formally inserted in the handle; very narrow, being at the broadest part hardly more than half an inch in breadth, but thick in proportion...

'A spear-head, or pike-head, was six or seven years ago amongst some old iron in a blacksmith's shop near to the field of battle, which was found on the field; it was purchased and taken away by a gentlemen. There is another curious relic of the battle, which has been preserved. A battle-axe, of which the blade is of small size; and the handle is perfect, of black oak, roughly made, and $2\frac{1}{2}$ inches in the gripe. The blade and handle of the axe, are together, about 18 inches long. Its history is curious. It was found very many years ago in the bed of the River Cock. (It was purchased by a Colonel Grant RA, who subsequently presented it to the Duke of Northumberland. It now resides in the museum at Alnwick Castle)...

'A spur which I have seen, of brass gilt, found on the field of battle is preserved in the Museum of the Society of Antiquaries of London; it is a rowel spur; the rowel is scarcely larger than a modern spur, in which respect it differs from the very large rowels, of that period, which have occasionally been discovered. The spur is remarkably perfect, and is slightly ornamented with a kind of scroll pattern. Upon the shanks is engraved in Old English characters the following inscription, *en loial amour, tout mon* coer, (meaning, 'all of my heart in loyal love'), the style and engraving of which, indicates its being of about the period of the battle.

'I also learnt, on my visit to Towton Field in 1854, that

on the recent occasion of making excavations for the York and North Midland Railway, close to Towton, some human bones were discovered; the spot was near the old road before described, and in the line of retreat of the Lancastrians from the field of battle, towards Tadcaster...'[18]

With the arrival of the metal detector, many more items such as arrow heads, buckles, studs and buttons have been found in more recent years, but to my knowledge, the only major find was a gauntlet ring – again said to have the insignia of the Percy family upon it. Prior to this, an interesting story did appear in the *Yorkshire Evening Post* on 20 April 1926, which read:

'£1,500 COLLAR FOUND AT TOWTON BATTLE RELIC; WOMAN RECALLS PLOUGHMAN'S TREASURE.

Mrs. Davis, a widow, now living in Hunslet, took an especial interest in the story of the battle of Towton because of her birth in Saxton village where her father, Mr. Edward Warrington, was the village shoemaker and also clerk and sexton at Saxton Parish Church. He had much to do with the restoration and proper preservation of Lord Dacre's tomb in the churchyard. Mrs. Davis is now 69, and we give the story as she tells it.

'I wrote to you about a supposed-to-be-brass ring', she said, 'which was turned up by the plough in one of the fields on Saxton Grange farm about 55 years ago. I could go very nearly blind-folded to the spot now. Mr. Henry Smart had the farm then, and I was a girl of about 14 working there. Tom Ambler, who came from Church Fenton, was there as second wagoner.

He ploughed this ring up in the field and said it would make a nice collar for the dog, a black retriever we had on the farm. I have put the collar on and off many a time. I called it a ring, but it was quite a big collar. It was all caked up and clogged, but as we brushed the dirt off it we found that it was made of moveable parts in such a way that when It was small – closed up like – it was broad, and as it stretched out it went narrower. It fastened with a sort of clasp.

It was a battle relic right enough. We thought it was just a brass collar at first and then one day Mr. Benjamin

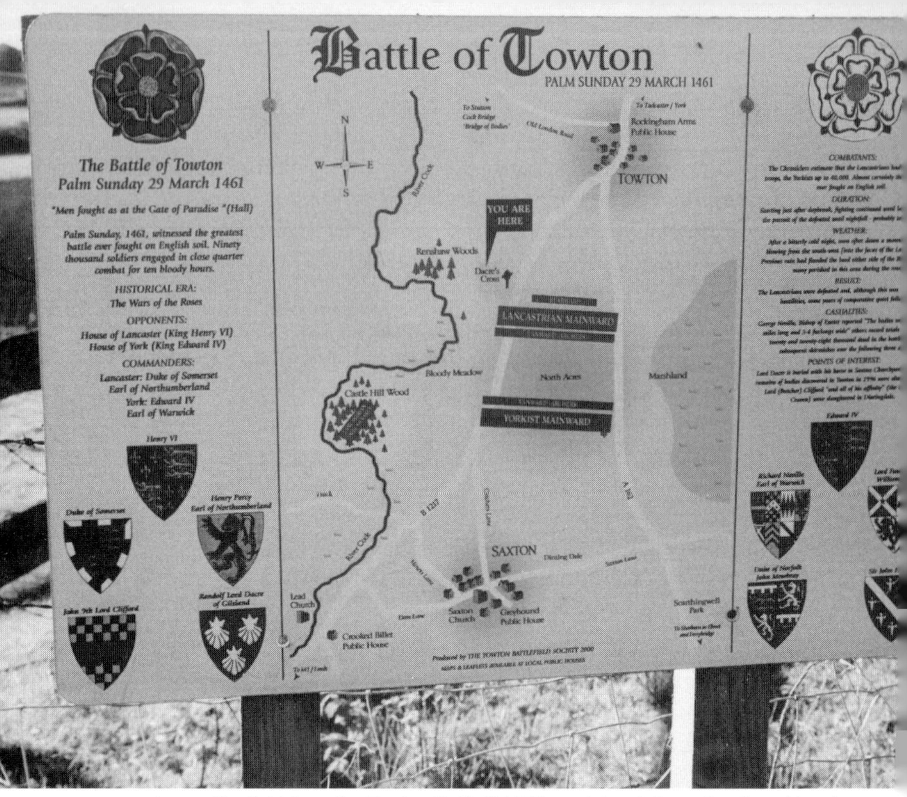

Across the field from the Towton Battlefield Memorial an information board has been set up by the Towton Battlefield Society. This board contains useful information in brief, easy to digest form.

Hey of Sherburn came shooting with Mr. Smart. They took the retriever with them and looking at the collar Mr. Hey asked where it came from and then said, 'I'll give you £5 for t'collar Harry.'

Mr Smart said, 'Nay, if its worth £5 to you its worth £5 to me,' and they began to examine it. The dog had been wearing it about eight months and it had begun to shine and some things on it which we took to be studs had begun to glitter. They turned out to be gems and rubies, and what we thought was brass was gold.

'I'd have it valued Harry,' said Mr. Hey, and they took it to York and the man they took it to offered them £600 for it straight away. They sold it and the last we heard of that collar was that it had been sold at one of the sale rooms in London for £1,000. I think it was at that place – you know Christies. And all that Tom Ambler, who ploughed it up got, was two pints of beer, I served him with it out of a barrel in the kitchen.' [19]

There is an irony in this story, in that it very much mirrors that of the Wakefield Sword, in so much as these very rare items – of so much interest to the battlefield historians and enthusiasts – are so often sold at auction, and are lost to the general public and never seen again.

Having now reviewed both the churchyard and considered what remnants of the soldiers, nobles and lords who fought in the mêlée itself have been discovered since that fateful day, we come to the end of our tour. The village of Saxton is a good place to bring it to a close, as just around the corner from Saxton Church is the Greyhound Inn public house, yet another excellent place to refresh ourselves and contemplate the events that led to and resulted from one of history's greatest military engagements.

A visit to the walls of City of York and the visitor attraction museum at Micklegat Bar – the scene of gruesome acts – will help round off the tou Here you may be help to capture the times when England had tw kings, and two feudin houses fought for supremacy in the Cou of Yorkshire.

Micklegate Bar, York

Chapter Notes

Chapter One

1.*London Chronicle for 1446 – 52*, p297 – 298.
2.*The Dijon Relation*, p63.
3.Davies, p95 – 97.
4.*Registrum Abbatie*,Whethamstede, p376 – 378.
5.Waurin, p315.
6.Goodman, *The Wars of the Roses*, p41.

Chapter Two

1.Greg, p208 – 210.
2.Hall, p249 – 250.
3.Vergil, p108.
4.Stow, p683 – 684.
5.Johnson, *Duke Richard Of York 1411 – 1460*, p218 – 219.
6.Davies, p106.
7.Hall, p250.
8.Worc, p484.

Chapter Three

1.Waurin, p326.
2.Stow, p683.
3.Davies, p106.
4.Markham, p112 – 113.
5.Hall, p249.
6.Hall, p249 – 250.
7.Stow, p683.
8.Leadman, p354.
9.Vergil, p108.
10.Hall, p250.
11.Waurin, p325 – 326.
12.Hall, p250.
13.Vergil p108.
14.Hall, p250.
15.Davies, p106.
16.Stanfield, p35 – 38.
17.Markham, p113 – 114.
18.Tyas, p59 – 60.
19.Brooke, p64 – 65.
20.Stanfield, p40 – 41.
21.Stanfield, p43.
22.Brooke, p59.
23.Hall p250 – 251.
24.Worc, p485.
25.Worc, *Annales Rerum Anglicarum*, Vol.II, ed Stevenson, 1884.
26.Leland, Vol. I, p43.
27.J W Walker, *St. Mary's Chapel on Wakefield Bridge*, Y.A.J, Vol.11,p154.
28.Barrett, p136 – 137.
29.Stanfield, p43 – 44.
30.Worc, p485.
31.Stow, p413.
32.Davies, p107.
33.Hall, p251.
34.Hall, p251.
35.Stow, p684.
36.Worc, p485.
37.Vergil, p 108.

Chapter Four

1.*Croyland Abbey Chronicle*, p531.
2.RPV. p463-7.
3.*The Great Chronicle of London*, p194 – 5.
4.Goodman, *The Wars of the Roses*, p42.
5.Boardman, *The Battle of Towton*, p46.
6.Rose of Rouen, *Archaeologica* XXIX p343 – 7.

Chapter Five

1.Hall, p255.
2.Hall, p254 – 5.
3.Hall, p255.
4.Greg, p216.
5.Hall, p254 5.
6.Hall, p255.
7.*Calendar of State Papers of Milan*, p61.
8.Waurin, p337 – 8.
9.Waurin, p338.

Chapter Six

1. Vergil, p110.
2. Waurin, p339 – 340.
3. Hall, p255.
4. Hall, p255.
5. Hall, p255.
6. Brooke, p94 – 95.
7. Waurin, p340.
8. Hearne's Fragment, as shown in *The Chronicles of the White Rose of York*, p9.
9. Gregory, p217-8.
10. *Croyland Abbey Chronicle*,p425.
11. *Calendar of State Papers of Milan*, p61 – 62.

Chapter Seven

1. H.C Haldane, *Relics of the Battle of Wakefield 1460*, Y.A.J, Vol. 22, p128.
2. *The Battle of Wakefield*, K Dockray/R Knowles, p27.
3. J W Walker , *St. Mary's Chapel on Wakefield Bridge*, Y.A.J, Vol. 11, p144 – 148.
4. J W Walker , *St. Mary's Chapel on Wakefield Bridge*, Y.A.J, Vol. 11, p159 – 165.
5. Brooke, p62.
6. Forrest, *The History of Knottingly*, 1871, p102.
7. Forrest, *The History of Knottingly*, 1871, p105.
8. Boardman, *The Battle of Towton*, p86 – 88.
9. Leland, p243.
10. Leland, p243.
11. Brooke, p100 – 101.
12. Brooke, p93 – 94.
13. Brooke, p112 – 113.
14. Brooke, p125 – 126.
15. Leland, p243.
16. Brooke, p97 – 98.
17. Brooke, p94 – 95.
18. *Yorkshire Evening Post* 20th April, 1926.

Appendix I

1. Leland, Vol I, fo6.

Appendix II

1. Waurin, p327.

Sources and References

Contemporary and near contemporary sources:

Fabyan, R.*The New Chronicles of England and France*, ed H.T. Ellis, 1811.

William Gregory *Gregory's Chronicle*, in *The Historical Collections of a Citizen of London*, ed J. Gairdner, C.S., 1876.

Edward Hall *Hall's Chronicle*, ed H. Ellis, 1809.

Thomas Hearne *Hearnes Fragment*, in *The Chronicles of the White Rose of York*, ed J. C. Giles, 1843.

John Leland *Itinenary*, 1558 – The Yorkshire extracts, as shown in Y.A.J, Vol. 10, 1889.

John Stow *Annales, or a Generall Chronicle of England*, (1615).

P. de Commines *Memoires*, ed J. Calmette and G. Durville, 3 Vols, *Les Classiques de l'historie de France au moyen*, Paris 1923 – 25

Polydore Vergil *Three Books of Polydore Vergil's English History*, ed Sir H. Ellis, C.S., 1844.

John Warkworth Warkworth Chronicle in *The Chronicle of the White Rose of York*, ed J. C. Giles, 1843.

William Worcestre *Annales Rerum Angelicarum*, Translation as shown in *The Chronicles of the White Rose of York*, LXXXIII, ed JC. Giles, 1843.

William Worcestre *Annales Rerum Angelicarum*, ed J. Stevenson, 1884.

William Worcestre *Itineraries* ed John H Harvey, Oxford, 1969.

John de Waurin *Recuil des Chroniques D' Engleterre*, eds W. Hardy & E. Hardy, 1891.

Whethamstede, J. *Registrum Abbatis*, ed H.T. Riley, 1872.

John Davies *An English Chronicle of the reigns of Richard II, Henry IV, V, VI* , C S., 1856.

William Gregory *Gregory's Chronicle*, in *The Historical Collections of a Citizen of London*, ed J. Gairdner, C.S., 1876.

Croyland Abbey Chronicle, ed Nicholas Proney and John Cox, Richard III & Yorkist History Trust, 1986.

Chronicle of the Rebellion in Lincolnshire, as shown in *Three Chronicles of the Reign of Edward IV*, C.S., C19.

Three fifteenth Century Chronicles, ed J. Gairdner, Camden Society, 1880.

Rotuli Parliamentorum, Vol V, VI, Record Commission.

Calendar of Charter Rolls, VI (1427 – 1516), 1927.

Calendar of Close Rolls, Edward IV, II, (1468 – 1476), 1953.

Calendar of Patent Rolls, Edward IV, II, (1467 – 1477), 1899.

The Great Chronicle of London, ed A. H. Thomas and I.D. Thornlry, 1938.

Calendar of State Papers and Manuscripts existing in the archives and collections of Milan, I, 1385 – 1618, ed AB Hinds.

Calendar of Close Rolls, Henry VI, (1454 – 1461), 1967.

Calendar of Patent Rolls, Henry VI, (1454 – 1461), 1911.

An English Chronicle of the reigns of Richard II, Henry IV, V, VI, ed John S

Davies, Camden Society, 1856.
York Civic Records, ed A. Raines, Y.A.S, Record Series, 98, 1939.
The Chronicles of the Wars of the Roses, ed Elizabeth Hallem, Weidenfeld and Nicholson, 1992.
Principal sources:
Barrett, CRB. *Battles and Battlefields in England*, Innes, 1896.
Boardman, A.*The Battle of Towton*, Sutton Publishing, 1993.
Brooke, R.*Visits to the Fields of Battles in England*, John Russell Smith, 1857.
Freeman, EA.*The Battles of Wakefield*, 1894.
Goodman, A.*The Wars of the Roses*, Routledge, 1981.
Haigh, PA.*The Battle of Wakefield 1460*, Sutton Publishing, 1996.
Johnson, PA. *Richard Duke of York, 1411 – 1460*, Oxford University Press, 1988.
Leadman, ADH.*The Battle of Wakefield*, Y.A.J, Vol. XI, 1891.
Markham, CR.*The Battle of Wakefield*, Y.A.J, Vol. IX, 1886.
Stanfield, A. Sandal Castle and the Battle of Wakefield. (A paper read before the Wakefield Photographic Society) 1891.
Tyas, G.*The Battles of Wakefield*, 1854.

Secondary sources:
Beesley, *A.History of Banbury, 1841.*
Bernard Saunders ,W. Fenland Notes and Queries, Vol I, Geo. C. Caster, 1891.
Budge, J.*Histories of the Parishes of Chipping Warden and Edgecote*, (Masters Dissertation) Loughborough University, 1992.
Butler, L.*Sandal Castle – Wakefield*, Wakefield Historical Society, 1991.
Burne, A. H.*Battlefields of England*, Methuen, 1950.
Burne, A. H.*More Battlefields of England*, Methuen, 1952.
Carpenter, C. *Locality and Polity*, Cambridge, 1992.
Crowther, G. H. *A Descriptive History of the Wakefield Battles*, 1886.
Crimes, S. B.Lancastrians, *Yorkists, and Henry VII*, London, 1964.
Drake, F. *Eboracum*, 1736.
Dockray, K. The Yorkshire Rebellions of 1469, *The Ricardian*, The journal of the Richard III Society, Vol VI, No 83, Dec 1983.
Evans, H. T. *Wales and the Wars of the Roses*, Sutton Publishing, 1995.
Forrest, C. *The History of Knottingly*, 1871.
Gairdner, J. *The Paston Letters*, Sutton Publishing, 1986.
Giles, J. C. *The Chronicles of the White Rose of York*, 1843.
Gillingham, J.*The Wars of the Roses*, Weidenfeld Paperbacks, 1990.
Gransden, A. *Historical Writings in England*, London, 1982.
Griffith, P. *The Battle of Blore Heath*, Paddy Griffith Associates, 1995.
Griffiths, R. A. *Local Rivalries and National Politics: The Percies and the Nevilles, and the Duke of Exeter, 1452 – 1455, Speculum 43*, 1968.
Haigh, P. A. *Military Campaigns of the War of the Roses*, Sutton Publishing, 1995.

Haigh,P. A. The Identity and Actions of Robin of Redesdale and Robin of Holderness, *Battlefield*, Vol 1, Battlefield Press, 1995.
Haigh, P. A. The 14th Lord of Winestead and the Battle of Towton, *Battlefield*, Vol 1 issue 1, Battlefield Press, 1995.
Haigh, P. A. Where Both the Hosts Fought, *Battlefield,* Battlefield Press, 1997.
Hammonds, P. W. *The Battles of Barnet and Tewkesbury*, Sutton Publishing, 1990.
Hicks, M. *False, Fleeting, Perjur'd Clarence,* Headstart Publishing, 1992.
Hicks, M. *Bastard Feudalism*, Longman Press, 1995.
Harris, M. D. *Coventry Leet Book or Mayor's Register*, (Early English Text Society Original Series) 1907 – 13.
Hildyard, M. T .*The Hildyards*, a privately published account of the family history of the Hildyards, 1994.
Hibberts, C. *Agincourt*, Windrush, 1995.
Hodges, G. *Ludford Bridge and Mortimer's Cross*, Longaston Press, 1989.
Holland, P. *The Lincolnshire Rebellion of March 1470*, EHR, 1988.
Jacob, E. F. *The 15th Century, Oxford History of England*, 1961.
Jones, Dr *York, Somerset and the Wars of the Roses,* E,H,R, 1989.
Jack, R. I. *The Battle of Northampton, July 10th 1460, Northamptonshire Past and Present* III, no I, 1960.
Kendall, P. M. *Warwick the Kingmaker and the Wars of the Roses*, Sphere Books, 1972.
Kinross, J. *Walking and Exploring the Battlefields of England*, Davis and Charles, 1993.
Kingsford, C. L. *English Historical Literature in the 15th Century*, Oxford, 1913.
Lander, J. R. *The Wars of the Roses*, Sutton Publishing, 1993.
Lander, J. R. *Crown and Nobility, 1450 – 1509, 1976.*
Lander, J. R. *Henry VI and the Duke of York's Second Protectorate*, B.J.R.L, XLIII, 1960.
Mc Farlane, K. B. *England in the Fifteenth Century*, Hambledon, 1981.
Miller, N. J. *Winestead and its Lords*, Brown and Son Ltd, 1932.
Oman, C Sir. *The Art of War in the Middle Ages*, Vol II, Greenhill Books, 1991.
Oman, C. Sir. *Warwick The Kingmaker*, 1891.
Pollard, R.A.J. *Percies and Nevilles*, History Today, Sept, 1993.
Powick, M. R. *Military Obligations in Medieval England*, Oxford University Press, 1962.
Poulson, G. *The History and Antiquities of the Seigniory of Holderness*, Vol II, Brown and Pickering, MDCCCXLI.
Ray, P. *English Civil War* – Notes and Queries, Vol. 44.
Ramsay, J Sir. *Lancaster and York*, Vol. II, Oxford, 1892.
Ross, C. *Edward IV*, Methuen, 1991.
Ross, C. *Richard III*, Methuen, 1988.
Ross, C. *The Estates and Finances of Richard Duke of York*, Welsh History

Review, III, 1967.
Ross, C. *The Wars of the Roses*, Thames and Hudson, 1986.
Rodgers, A. T*he Making of Stamford*, Leicester University Press, 1965.
Rodgers, A. *The Book of Stamford*, Barracuda, 1983.
Smurthwaite, D. *Complete Guide to the Battlefields of Britain*, Mermaid Books, 1993.
Scofield, C. L. *The Life and Reign of Edward IV*, Vol. I, 1923.
Speed, J. *The Counties of Britain, A Tudor Atlas* by John Speed, 1988.
Story, R. L. *The End of the House of Lancaster*, Barrie and Rockliff, 1966.
Storey, R. L. *Lincolnshire and the Wars of the Roses*, 1966.
Storey, R. L. *The North of England in Fifteenth Century England*, ed Chrimes, Ross, and Griffiths, 1972.
Thomas, D. H. *The Herberts of Raglan and the battle of Edgecote 1469*, Freezywater Publications, 1994.
Wolffe, B. *Henry VI*, Methuen, 1983.
Walker , J. W. *St. Mary's Chapel on Wakefield Bridge*, Y.A.J, Vol. 11. Dockray/Knowles *The Battle of Wakefield,* 1993.
Hammond/Sutton/Visser – Fuchs *The Reburial of Richard Duke of York 21-30 July 1476*, 'The Ricardian', Vol. X, No 127, 1994.

Appendix I

The burial of the Duke of York

The Duke of York's death upon the battlefield of Wakefield, in the 49th year of his life, was the most significant consequence of that particular Wars of the Roses conflict. However, he was not afforded a state funeral until 1476, sixteen years after his death.

Following the battle of Towton the heads of the slain Yorkist leaders, which had been placed on the walls and gates of York, were – due to the pressing needs to continue the campaign against the surviving Lancastrians in Northumberland – quickly interred where their bodies lay at Pontefract. Their funerals were planned to take place at a later date when there were less demanding issues to deal with.

It was not until five years after the turbulent period which witnessed the rebellions of 1469 and 1470 and the battles of Barnet and Tewkesbury, when Edward IV had fully established a stable kingdom, that the final burial took place. The body of the Duke of York was exhumed from its temporary grave in the grounds of St. Richard's Friary, 20 or 21 July 1476, in readiness for the journey to its final resting place at the family home of Fotheringhay. In getting there, the route that the funeral entourage was to take was as follows:

Sunday 21 July, it remained at Pontefract, where prayers were said all day in memory of the Duke of York and the Earl of Rutland.

Monday 22 July it was moved the fourteen miles to Doncaster.

Tuesday, 23 July it made the journey the twelve miles to Blyth,.

Wednesday 24 July, it was moved the fifteen miles to Tuxford.

Thursday 25 July, it was conveyed the eleven miles to Newark.

Friday 26 July, it was moved the thirteen miles to Grantham.

Saturday 27 July it travelled twenty miles to Stamford – where it remained on Sunday 28 July, and where again, there was a day of prayer.

Monday 29, the journey finished when the entourage arrived at Fotheringhay at between two and three in the afternoon.

It was taken to Fotheringhay in a specially commissioned hearse, which cost £75 17s 2d, and was built by one John Talbot of London. Planning the event was a major logistical achievement. Preparations were made for the resting places for the coffins of York and his son Rutland at the end of each day. Equally, other nobles who were not making the actual journey to Fotheringhay had to be informed of the route that the funeral entourage would be taking, so that they and their households could join the funeral party while it was enroute, in order to pay their respects. The funeral party itself was escorted from Pontefract by many of the leading nobles of the realm (including some whose ancestors were involved in York's death).

This party included: Henry Percy, Earl of Northumberland, Thomas,

Lord Stanley, Richard Hastings, Lord Welles, Ralph, Lord Greystoke, Humphrey, Lord Dacre and John Blount, Lord Mountjoy. The young Duke of Gloucester the late Duke of York's third surviving son and later Richard III – walked solemnly before his father's funeral entourage all the way to Fotheringhay, where Edward IV soberly awaited their arrival with an even more impressive collection of nobles, including his brother the Duke of Clarence, John de la Pole, Earl of Lincoln, Henry Bourchier, Earl of Essex, Edmund Grey, Earl of Kent, Anthony Woodville, Earl Rivers, William, Lord Hastings, Walter Devereux, Lord Ferrers and James Touchet, Lord Audley and many more.

The actual funeral took place on Tuesday 30 July and was (along with other festivities) attended by over 2,000 people. Contemporary and near contemporary accounts of the Duke of York's funeral are few and far between, however, with reference to the duke's body being exhumed and subsequently buried at Fotheringhay, Leland mentioned this as follows:

> '...caused the body of his (Edward IV's) father to be brought from Pontefract thither (Fotheringhay) and layid to rest on the north side of the Highe Altare...'

The Duchess of York who died thirty years after the Duke of York, and who survived all her children bar one, (she died at Berkhamsted on 31 May 1495), was buried alongside her husband at Fotheringhay.

In reference to this, Leland also chronicled the following:

> '...where is also buried, King Edward IV's mother, in a vaulte, over the which is a pratie chappelle...' (6)

After the battle of Wakefield, the Neville family also took time to mourn the loss of the Earl of Salisbury and Sir Thomas Neville, and the bodies of father and son were, with equal solemnity, finally laid to rest at Bisham Abbey in Buckinghamshire, on 15 January 1463, at a funeral which was attended by all the Neville adherents, while the House of York was represented by George, Duke of Clarence and the Elizabeth, Duchess of Suffolk.

Fotheringay Castle, family home of the House of York.

Appendix II

Recruitment of soldiers in the Wars of the Roses

In the middle ages there were two main methods of recruiting troops. The first was 'livery and maintenance', and can be explained as follows. During the Hundred Years War, there was a large standing English army brought about by contract through the nobles of the land who paid for their services and supplied captains to control and direct them. However, as the Hundred Years Wars came to an end the need for a large standing army diminished; in fact, during the Wars of the Roses, the official English army consisted only of the Calais garrison – which protected the sole remaining English possession in France at that time.

This meant that during the late 1450s and early 1460s there were to be found considerable numbers of unemployed professional soldiers roaming the kingdom with little work skills, and little desire to seek alternative livings. These ex men-at-arms went on to find employment in the service of powerful English nobles who could afford to retain their services. Consequently, the likes of the Earl of Northumberland and the Earl of Warwick amassed large, equipped and liveried, personal armies. Their services to their lord was in return for the lord's protection in matters of life, such as legal issues for example.

The lords in turn owed allegiance to the sovereign who could call on them and their private armies in times of need. With respect to the Wars of the Roses it was a matter of personal loyalty and feeling which swayed a lord between one king or another – or in the case of the Battle of Wakefield – the king, Henry VI, and the pretender, Richard Duke of York. Summoning these lords to assist in a likely cause was usually achieved by written communication as the following shows. This is a letter from the Duke of Norfolk to the Pastons asking them to join with him for Richard III, against Henry Tudor at the time of the battle of Bosworth:

> '...and that ye bring with you such a company of tall men as ye may goodly make at my cost and charge and I pray you ordain them jackets of my livery, and I shall content you at your meeting with me.' [1]

In this event, the Pastons chose to ignore the request.

The second way of recruiting men was by 'Commission of Array' which worked in the following manner: A king (or protector) could issue a commission of array to any noble, which in effect meant that the recipient noble could recruit in the king's name and on his behalf, the men from the shires between the age of sixteen and sixty in the defence of the realm.

This usually meant that a central gathering point would be assigned and that the levies would be required to attend at a given time. Therefore messages had to be sent around the shires informing people of the muster, and time allowed for the gathering. This method of recruiting from the shires was Anglo Saxon in origin, but in calling upon the levies of the shire the response was dependent on the individual levies' strength of allegiance to the king. Although, to fail in answering this summons was for the levies, in some instances, punishable by death, this form of summons, nevertheless, on occasion went unanswered.

A good example of a commission which can still be seen today is the Bridport Muster Roll, which formed part of a Commission of Array in 1457. In this particular muster some 12,000 men were gathered from southern England for Henry VI. It is interesting to note that in trying to discover who was present at a battle during the Wars of the Roses, the probability of discovering a single muster roll for either side is unlikely. In the course of each side raising an army, a number of commissions would have been used as outlined above, thus several sources (or muster rolls), would have to be consulted to discover a single army's composition at a given period of time. For further details regarding recruitment I suggest that the following is consulted, M. Hicks, *Bastard Feudalism*, Longman 1995, and C. Carpenter, *Locality and Polity*, Cambridge, 1992. A concise account of recruiting – which is easy to read and understand bearing in mind the complexity of the subject – can be found in both A. W. Boardman's, *The Battle of Towton 1461*, (pages 55-57) and section two of Goodman's, *The Wars of the Roses*, particularly chapter six, 'Military Convention and Recruitment'.

ROYAL ARMOURIES, LEEDS

Mediaeval display of weapons, armour and military clothing as worn for the Battle of Towton. Crossbow range, dramatic interpretations and live action events. Allow at least four hours.

Royal Armouries Museum, Leeds SLS10 1LT
Telephone: 0990 1066 66
opening times:
Monday to Sunday 10.30am - 5.30pm (4.30pm Nov. to Mar.)

SANDAL CASTLE

A Visitor Centre will be opening in the summer of 2002.

Manygates Lane, off Barnsley Road, Wakefield
Telephone enquiries to: 01924 305352
Castle opening times: Daily dawn to dusk
(Car park 9.30 am to dusk)

PONTEFRACT CASTLE

A Lancastrian stronghold during the early days of the Wars of the Roses from whence a strong force set out to attack the Duke of York ensconced at Sandal in the days following Christmas 1460. By March 1461 Pontefract Castle had gone over to the Yorkist cause and served as a base prior to the Battle of Towton. The castle figured largely during the Civil War.

Castle Chain, Pontefract, West Yorkshire WF8 1QH
Telephone: 01977 723440
Castle opening times:
Monday to Friday 8.30am - 6.45pm (dusk in Winter)
Saturday and Sunday 10.30 - 6.45pm (dusk in Winter)
Visitor Centre: open as part of Magazine tour

WAKEFIELD MUSEUM

Following your visit to the ruins of Sandal Castle take a trip into Wakefield to the museum where artifacts discovered from excavations at the mediaeval stronghold are on display.

Wood Street, Wakefield, West Yorkshire WF1 2EW
Telephone: 01924 305356
opening times:
Monday to Saturday 10.30am - 4.30pm
Sunday 2.00 - 4.30pm

CONISBROUGH CASTLE

The grandest room in the castle – The Lord's Hall.

Conisbrough Castle & Visitor Centre, Castle Hill, Conisbrough, Doncaster DN12 3BU. Telephone 01709 863329 Situated between Doncaster and Rotherham just off the A630. Open 10.00am - 5.00pm (4.00pm in Winter). A small admission charge.

Conisbrough became a royal castle when Edward IV became king in 1461. The gardrobe, or royal toilet, leading off from the Lord's Hall.

THE CITY OF YORK

Mediaeval buildings and museums:
Barley Hall, Coffee Yard, Off Stonegate, York YO1 2AW;
Merchant Aventurers' Hall, Fossgate, York YO1 2XD;
Treasurer's House, Minister Yard, York YO1 7JQ
Micklegate Bar exhibition.
Monk Bar Richard III exhibition.
Yorkshire Museum, Museum Gardens, York YO1 7FR

Monk Bar no longer has a barbican but still retains its working portcullis.

Great Hall of the Merchant Adventurers' Company, founded in 1357.

SKIPTON CASTLE

This is among the best preserved mediaeval castles in England. A Lancastrian stronghold and home of John Clifford, 9th Lord of Skipton ('The Butcher') who killed the young Earl of Rutland on Wakefield Bridge. See pages 46 and 108.

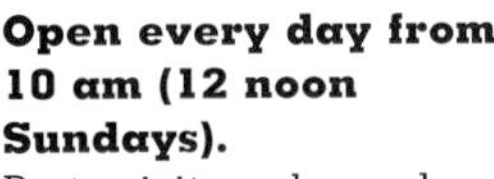

Open every day from 10 am (12 noon Sundays).
Party visits welcomed.
Small admission fee.

Coat of Arms of John Lord Clifford, nicknamed the 'Butcher' following his merciless slaying of Edmund. Clifford motto: 'DESORMAIS' (Henceforth).

Steps leading to the dungeons at Skipton Castle.

KNARESBOROUGH CASTLE

Mediaeval royal castle overlooking the River Nydd. A Lancastrian stronghold with some interesting features, including dungeons.

Opening times: Good Friday – end of September daily 10.30am to 5pm

BATTLEFIELDS TRUST

The Battlefields Trust is dedicated to the preservation, interpretation and presentation of battlefields as educational and heritage resources. It runs a membership scheme, with subscriptions running for one year from the date of joining. The ordinary subscription rate is currently £15.00. Members receive the quarterly journal *Battlefield*, which includes the newsletter of the Trust, as well as reduced rates of Battlefields Trust events, including Study Days, walks and conferences. Members automatically become members of their local branch. Full details of the Battlefields Trust can be found on their website: www.battlefieldstrust.com or from the Co-ordinator, Michael Rayner, at 33 High Green, Brooke, Norwich, NR15 1HR. Telephone/fax: 01508 558145. Email: BattlefieldTrust@aol.com

TOWTON BATTLEFIELD SOCIETY

The Society was formed to promote the permanent preservation of the land area where the bloodiest battle ever fought on English soil occurred.

Also the Society is committed to an education programme to bring a public awareness to the significance of the Battle of Towton. For some reason the battle where two rival kings faced each other (although Henry VI, for Lancaster, personally remained in the City of York) is not so readily acknowledged and taught as some battles and battle sites in this country.

Associated activities include: Research, Period Costume, Archery and Heraldry.

The Society meets on the first Monday of each month at Saxton Village Hall at 7.30.

All who have an interest in the preservation and investigation of the longest fought battle, and by far the most expensive in human lives, ever to have taken place in England, are encouraged to join the Society.

Membership fee details from: Mr P A Hetherington, 15 Heathercroft, Brockfield Park, Huntington, York YO31 9EG

CONISBROUGH & DENABY MAIN HERITAGE GROUP

Formed for futherment of local history matters. Membership is open to all ages and all are welcome to attend the monthly meetings, which are held on the first Thursday in the month.

Telephone 01709 324702 for venue, times and details of speakers.

THE RETINUE OF SIR THOMAS STANLEY

A re-enactment, living history society, offering educational services to schools and youth organisations. This takes the form of an authentic display of life in the mediaeval period based around life in a tented campaign village, which includes costume, furniture and crafts from the period of the Wars of the Roses. Drills, archery, arms, armour and fighting techniques are exhibited and demonstrated.

They are regularly involved in galas, fetes and carnivals. Displays are tailored to fit the requirements of the function organisers.

The Society meets and trains every Monday evening at Rawmarsh Leisure Centre, near Rotherham. New members are always welcome.

Contact: Bob Bridge *Promotions Officer*
The Retinue of Sir Thomas Stanley,
83 St Johns Road, Rotherham S65 1LT
Telephone 07980 163484

The author may be contacted at:
phil@haighpfsworld.co.uk

The author, Philip A Haigh, at the site of the Battle of Wakefield, November 2001.

INDEX

Y